KT-161-584

BACK DROPS
pages from a private diary

By the same Author
Acid Drops

KENNETH WILLIAMS

BACK DROPS
pages from a private diary

DRAWINGS BY LARRY

J M Dent & Sons Ltd
London Melbourne Toronto

First published 1983
© Kenneth Williams 1983
Illustrations © 'Larry' 1983

All rights reserved. No part of this
publication may be reproduced, stored in
a retrieval system, or transmitted, in any form or by
any means, electronic, mechanical, photocopying,
recording or otherwise, without the prior
permission of J M Dent & Sons Ltd

This book is set in 12/14 point VIP Sabon by
D. P. Media Limited, Hitchin, Hertfordshire

Printed and bound in Great Britain by Biddles Ltd,
Guildford, Surrey for
J M Dent & Sons Ltd
Aldine House, 33 Welbeck Street, London W1M 8LX

British Library Cataloguing in Publication Data

Williams, Kenneth
    Back drops.
    I. Title
    828'.91407   PR6061.I/
    ISBN 0-460-04583-0

Foreword

It will not be news to anyone in the theatre that a back drop denotes a change of scene, and as a retrospective look at events is to drop back on the past, so *Back Drops* suits this collection of diary entries culled from my most recent volume.

The idea grew out of the success of a BBC radio programme about diaries in which I read some extracts, which were then also chosen for the Pick of the Week spot. Several people suggested later 'Why not make a book of the journal?' I demurred at first. I felt that the reason the broadcast succeeded was that the items were selected; to publish a fuller diary would be indiscreet.

Well, my publishers – or at least their lawyers – have dealt with the indiscretions, so here we are. Apart from altering one or two names and dates (to protect the innocent and confuse the enemy) I have not tampered with the original in any way. *Back Drops* is quite simply edited highlights from a year in the life of yours truly,

KENNETH WILLIAMS

For Stanley and Moira

January

1 January

The start of another year. Walking through Regent's Park this morning, past the barren trees, I reflected that I couldn't turn over a new leaf since there wasn't one to be seen. A passer-by, wearing a radio head-set, called out, 'Hello, how's it going, Kenny?' I smiled mutely, not knowing *what* was supposed to be going, nor where it was going to, unless it was humanity going up to the Gates of Heaven in a formless din. Perhaps we should all start wearing head-sets.

In the evening to Barry Wade's party in his new flat. Everyone murmured admiration for the bric-à-brac. Miriam Karlin told me about her own house-warming party. 'I invited quite a lot of people for drinks in the new house,' she said, 'and Fenella Fielding went all over the place inspecting every room. Finally she returned and pronounced judgement: "It's a great success, darling, when are you going to bring it into town?" '

My sinus congestion got worse during the party, the remnants of the Christmas cold. 'I suppose I'll have to go back to that ENT man,' I said despairingly to Barry, 'and have it cauterized.'

'How on earth do they do that?' he asked.

'They burn through the nasal passages to allow the air in,' I said. 'It's a dreadful, painful process. They bore right through both nostrils.'

'Get some menthol and shove a couple of pipe cleaners up instead,' he laughed, 'then you won't be paying through the nose.'

On the way home I reflected that Barry always did have very little understanding of rhinology.

4 January

Bronchial condition still painful. Must have been mad to look for electric food-mixers in the afternoon, especially as the shops were bedlam with sales customers. The noise in Harrods merely increased the agony.

Met Michael for dinner at The Hungry Horse. He talked about a company trip to the Far East. 'It's going to be a lot of fun, with a lot of parties,' he said.

'If you're going to meet people in the East and have any kind of adventures with them,' I told him, 'you'll really need someone to teach you the techniques required for oriental love-making. They're quite different from European styles. You'll need to find some Mandarin expert on all the social and sexual customs of the East.'

'Yes, I suppose I'd need to,' he said pensively, 'otherwise I'd be a bull in a china shop.'

I laughed immoderately, but he seemed totally unaware that he had made a witticism. Odd that a lot of the best lines are unconsciously funny – like the French lady who said, 'I wish for a penis,' until she was enlightened by a friend, who said 'In English, it's pronounced *happiness*.'

5 January

In Dr Clarke's waiting-room I sat next to a man with a Sherlock Holmes hat and a very nasty cold. When I went in to see Bertie (Clarke) I said, 'That man in the deer-stalker has been giving me his germs.'

'Don't worry,' he said. 'I've filled him so full of penicillin that every time he sneezes, he cures everyone in the room.' *Very* droll I thought – for a doctor.

I told him the bronchitis had left me feeling tired and

wan. 'Only the other night, I fell asleep watching television', I said.

'I'm not surprised,' he said, 'watching all that rubbish.' He then gave me a prescription for iron tablets. 'In the old days you got iron naturally in black bread. But now everyone eats the white stuff.'

Taking his tip I stopped on the way home at the health shop. A sympathetic assistant sold me a loaf made with real wheatgerm. 'These modern bakers', she said, 'take all the good things out of the flour and sell them on the side. They call them by-products and flog what's left over, but it's all soggy rubbish that tastes like blotting paper. They publicize white bread as being pure. The English have always had a thing about purity and whiteness. Have you noticed how we put our brides in white, how our underwear's white, our hospitals are white — it's no wonder we end up looking white ourselves. We walk around as white as sheets. If anyone takes a holiday in France, where you can still get black bread, they come back and get stared at. People cry out, "Oh, you do look brown! Have you been on holiday?" It's finally got through to the British that if you look well, you must have been abroad, enjoying the sunshine and natural food.'

'Very perceptive,' I said. 'You should be lecturing on nutrition.'

'Ah,' she smiled, 'but then I'd never meet charmers like you!'

'Flattery will get you anywhere,' I said, repressing my blushes.

7 January

Heard Bernard Cribbins on LBC. I telephoned the station and they broadcast our chat together. I reminded him of the time when the cordite singed him on the behind in *Carry on Spying*. That reminded him in turn of a sketch he did in revue. He had to sit on a throne in great magnificence as four trumpeters appeared and played a fanfare which went on and on. When it finally stopped Bernard said, 'You fools, I ordered crumpets.'

I wished him a Happy New Year, and rang off.

10 January

To Brian and Molly Dobson for dinner. Richard Williams was there, too. He directed me in my first animation film called *Love Me, Love Me*: I remember seeing it at the Academy some years ago.

I commented on the fact that Molly had given her children their meal earlier, on the grounds that it was better for children to eat before the adults.

Richard remarked, 'It's ridiculous, they're adults really. They've just shrivelled a bit, that's all.'

An animated wit, too, I see.

12 January

Bumped into Johnny Koon, the restaurateur, and we talked about the time when I'd been stranded in Gibraltar en route for Morocco. I was staying at the Queen's Hotel and having a drink in the bar when I met two men, whom I assumed at first were fellow-travellers, stranded as I was. When we got talking, however, one turned out to be a signalman on the aircraft-carrier *Eagle*, and the other a leading stoker. As they were dressed in civvies, I'd mistaken them for holidaymakers. While we were chatting the page came up and said, 'You're wanted on the phone.'

It was Johnny Koon: 'I'm opening my new Chinese

restaurant', he said, 'and I'd love it if you would come and cut the ribbon and make a little speech. *The Times of Gibraltar* will be taking pictures and I've invited the Governor and the C-in-C Troops, Gibraltar.'

I told him I'd just met two chums in the bar and he said, 'Bring them along – the more the merrier!'

We arrived at this grand restaurant opening. I spoke a few words of welcome to everyone, with a passing reference to the exotic nature of the East coming to Gibraltar, and then we were shown to our tables.

I found myself seated, with my signalman and stoker, opposite the Governor, the Admiral and their captain. I asked him the name of his ship. When he replied, 'The *Eagle*', I said 'Well, you'll know Sylvester and James here.'

The captain looked rather coldly at me and said, 'There are over two thousand men under my command, and it's hardly likely I would remember every face.'

I said, 'No, but as Dr Johnson rightly remarked, "When it comes to lapidary inscriptions, no man is upon oath".'

'Yes, that is very true,' he said uncertainly. 'How very wise, how very apt.' I secretly thought it wasn't apt at all, but it had filled what could have been an embarrassing gap.

A drink or two later, the page from the hotel rushed in to tell me that my plane was at last ready to go, and that my luggage had already been taken to the airport. I leapt up and bade a hasty farewell to my fellow-guests. But the Admiral stopped me and asked, 'What about transport?'

'Well, I assume I'll get a taxi in the street,' I said.

'No, don't worry,' he said, 'use my car.'

So I arrived at the airport in a huge Rolls Royce, flying the Admiral's pennant. The car drove straight onto the tarmac by the stairs up to the plane. The BEA staff were on the steps as the limousine arrived. Their faces were eager with expectation and awe at this unexpected VIP, and then I stepped out.

'Oh, it's that twit from the *Carry On's*,' a steward said. 'I suppose you'll want the gin and tonic.'

I doubt if even Dr Johnson would have had an answer to that one.

14 January

The Lyric, Hammersmith, rang about casting the part of the father in my production of *Entertaining Mr Sloane*. 'See if you can get David Blake Kelly,' I said. Within a few minutes they rang back to say that David would be delighted to accept. So that's more or less fixed all the casting for the play — except for the part of Cathy.

I mentioned this to Barbara Windsor, since I think she'd be marvellous in it. In discussing the kind of clothes that Cathy would wear Barbara had the temerity to reprove me, saying, 'I saw you the other day from the window of Hartnell's where I get my clothes. You were passing by and several of the assistants commented on your awful appearance — going around in that terrible, dirty old raincoat and filthy cap. You look like some old flasher. Can't you buy yourself some decent gear? You look as though you're dressed by Oxfam. If you tried, you could look quite smart.'

'Dressing smartly is not my style, Barbara'.

'As far as clothes are concerned, Kenneth, you haven't got *any* style,' she said.

Just as well Barbara and I are old chums. Anyway, we've fixed a meeting to discuss the part. When I said, 'Don't worry, I'll wear the right dress,' she said, 'Hang on, I think I prefer the raincoat.'

15 January

Hearing a radio talk today on the ludicrous nature of lines taken out of context made me remember the actor who took part in a documentary programme apropos of Regency Brighton and the Prince Regent's lavish entertaining in that daft pavilion. He had to say the line, 'The Prince Regent's balls were the largest in Europe.' He told me afterwards that there wasn't one note of complaint.

Trevor Baxter once told me about playing Robert Burns in an ill-fated production, where his opening gambit was, 'You'll excuse my crutch, Miss Maclehose?'

The Listener once printed a piece from a broadcast by the scientist, Brian Ford, who said, 'In Delhi I was taken to Dikshit University and passed by Phuket Island on my way through Malaysia, and in the South Pacific I learned that the Tongan for beautiful is "U-fukofa'ofa".'

Obviously, in the Orient, beauty is in the ear of the beholder – and the genteel will be supplied with ear-plugs.

16 January

Went to the Lyric, Hammersmith. Odd to think I shall be directing a play in the refurbished theatre where I made my debut in a musical, *The Buccaneer*, by Sandy Wilson. The place is full of curious memories for me. I was once taken by Eric Portman to see a revue there. During the interval I went to the lavatory, fell asleep on the seat, and woke up just in time to return for the National Anthem. 'Sorry' I whispered to E.P. 'I went right off!' 'Don't worry,' he returned drily, 'so did the show', which left me feeling quite guiltless.

The only other time I played the Lyric was in *Share My Lettuce*, before it transferred to the West End. In the

'Wallflower Waltz' scene, all the men danced with pieces of chiffon which floated down from the flies, while the girls stood apart, singing an accompaniment. On the first night, my piece of chiffon got caught on a spot-bar and I had nothing to dance with, so I spent the entire scene trying to steal pieces of material belonging to the others. They kept pushing me off, and I ran round from one to another muttering, 'I haven't got a bit!' It provoked so much laughter from the audience that this hitherto plaintive number in the show became a comedy item.

I told Roy Castle about this experience when I did 'Record Breakers' with him on television. We agreed that the unexpected can sometimes have very funny results in the theatre. 'I remember being on a bill with Tommy Cooper', Roy said, 'and commenting on the shortness of his turn that evening. Tommy said it was because he'd built the act round a walking stick, which was an essential prop, but the preceding artists had bolted their equipment to the floor and unbeknown to him there were now several holes in the stage. His walking stick fell through one of these and he was left with nothing to finish his act. Tommy didn't worry, though. He did a brilliant ad-lib, he said. He walked off!'

Then I told Roy about the funny ad-lib which occurred during the Equity AGM at the Victoria Palace when Dulcie Gray rose to complain, 'Mister Chairman, I must protest! There is no paper in the ladies' lavatory!' When someone grumbled, 'This is holding up the motion!' a wag shouted from the back, 'So is the lack of loo paper!'

In the evening to Richard Williams's studio to work on his new animated film, *The Thief and the Cobbler*. Richard said he'd got Vincent Price for the King and I told him how brilliant Vincent had been in *Champagne for Caesar*. 'If you ever get a chance to see that film, don't miss it!' I said. 'It's a marvellous satire on commercialism and sponsored broadcasting. In it there's a splendid line when, during a quiz game, Ronald Colman is asked: "What is the Japanese for goodbye?" and he says "Sayonara, not to be confused with Cyanide, which is goodbye in any language!" '

17 January

Dinner with John Schlesinger and Noel Davis. It seems extraordinary that my friendship with John stems from the transit camp at Nee Soon in Malaya in 1946. Even then John's flair for direction and his imaginative grasp of stage settings were obvious. We talked endlessly about our time with CSE (Combined Services Entertainment) in Singapore and I reminded him of the occasion when the sergeant-major committed suicide because he'd been discovered embezzling the funds and splitting the proceeds with the Chinese tailors who made the costumes.

The commanding officer paraded us and said, 'You've all heard the news. The sergeant-major's killed himself and now the man's more bloody trouble dead than he was alive. We've got to bury him. All those over six feet, stand forward for pall-bearing.' People shrank visibly in the ranks.

The colonel went down the line and stopped in front of Stanley Baxter, 'You'll do,' he said. 'Stand forward.'

'Ah, I'm sorry,' said Stanley, 'Church of Scotland.'

'Oh, I beg your pardon – of course,' said the colonel, and went on down the line. When he'd got past a few more the penny dropped. He turned back and said, 'Just a minute. What are you talking about, Church of Scotland? You bury people, don't you?'

Stanley spluttered, 'We-ell, yes, but. . . .'

'You'll do,' said the colonel. 'You'll go.'

So Stanley and the other members of the burial party were sent off to the British Military Cemetery in the midst of a tropical downpour. It was an ill-assorted group to lower a coffin. As well as Stanley, there was a pianist, a dancer, a pipe-major and a couple of others. They were all quite unmilitary. When they got there, they draped the coffin with a Union Jack, but the chaplain whispered, 'Get the flag off. It's ignominious death, no battle honours are given.'

Hurriedly the monsoon-sodden flag was removed and the service began. As the chaplain came to the passage about life being brief and full of misery, with the colonel standing, saluting reverently, a huge Cadillac drew up. A Chinese chauffeur got out and held up an umbrella for an attractive woman, visibly tearful, who came and stood alongside Stanley and the others.

'My dear,' whispered the Colonel, 'are you a friend of the deceased?'

'Friend?' she said in a pronounced American accent. 'I'm his wife.'

Stanley said they were all taken aback at the dead sergeant-major's secret nuptials. But the colonel sized up the situation promptly. At the end of the funeral he said, 'Dismiss your chauffeur, my dear. You are obviously distressed and in need of comfort. I will take you back to Nee Soon in my jeep.' And off they drove together.

I asked Stanley about the outcome. 'When I went in to see the Colonel for orders the next morning.' he said, 'there was the late sergeant-major's wife sitting in a kimono, sipping coffee! Never had the effects of mourning evaporated so rapidly.'

18 January

I'm reading the John Lahr biography of Joe Orton. Strange how Lahr's accounts of events I thought I'd remembered well are not at all as I had imagined them. Recalling my conversations with Joe during the tour of

Loot I'd have said that we got on very well with each other, but Lahr has found a letter from Orton complaining about my being temperamental! Can you imagine? Certainly Joe conveyed nothing of the kind to me. Of course one knows that people say contradictory things the moment one's back is turned, but it's still a shock to find that people one thinks of as constant and consistent are really mercurial and changeful. Perhaps we always expect too much of other people and are always disappointed by them. It's in the nature of humanity. That's why we need faith so much: the unaltering, the everlasting and the endlessly forgiving. I think of Wilfred Owen's line about 'the eternal reciprocity of tears.' The mind that can resolve contented thought is just as capable of harbouring discontent and despair.

I remember visiting Tony Hancock in hospital and finding the bed covered with books by Leibnitz, Nietzsche and Bertrand Russell. He said, 'I'm trying to discover the purpose of it all. Have you ever thought, Kenny, what if there's no point to existence at all? What if there's no one up there? Sometimes I think it's all a joke.'

'Well, in that case,' I said, 'you must try and make it a good one.'

'Oh, that's just evading the issue,' he said, and he went on to talk about the fictitious line we draw between subjectivity and objectivity. It's weird how people love definitions and labels; yet they so often turn out to be spurious – like the Motorist and the Pedestrian. Both labels are invalid; when the motorist gets out of his car he becomes a pedestrian and vice versa.

It's like the man searching under the lamp-post. A policeman asks what he's lost, and the man tells him he's dropped a coin 'over there', pointing to a spot in the darkness. 'Then why aren't you looking there?' asks the policeman.

'Because this is where the light is.'

25 January

With Michael to the Chanterelle restaurant. It was 12.15, but it was closed, so I banged on the door and the boy who admitted us said, quite distantly. 'We don't open until one on Sundays.' I swept him aside. We had a fairly good meal at all events, certainly a lot better than the disastrous one we had there the last time. Michael took me through a car-wash afterwards, which was quite an adventure. Barbara Windsor telephoned with the good news that she's going to play Cathy in *Sloane*. She told me she'd got three more weeks' panto in Newcastle and that business was marvellous. 'We're Harry Packers,' she said. She's staying at the Holiday Inn up there and said that she had done one length in its swimming pool.

'Rather you than me,' I said. 'You can pick up things in those places.'

'I've never heard that.'

'Well, you wouldn't. The p is silent as in pneumonia.'

We went on to discuss characterizations in general and how one approaches a role. Whenever I get on to that subject I'm always reminded of the person who rang up Alec Guiness, when he was rehearsing *Hamlet*, and said he'd discovered a completely original conception of the role in a wonderful book. Alec said, 'I'd be interested to read it. What is the book?'

'I can't remember the author,' said the caller.

'What's the title?'

'Well, I can't remember that either, but it was a red book.'

I related this to Barbara, who snorted derisively: 'Yes, advice like that is about as effective as a fart in wet blancmange.'

26 January

Hearing a Liszt recital on the radio today my mind drifted back to a revue I once did at the Duke of York's and to one night in particular when the stage-box was occupied by a gentleman who fell about laughing every time I was on. He laughed so much and so loudly that he nearly had us all giggling on the stage. The crisis came with the barber's sketch in which I was supposed to do elaborate things with Lance Percival's hair, while he expostulated, 'Nothing fancy, you understand. Just short back and sides.'

I had to rant on saying, 'Oh, I've had them all in here. I've had bishops in here. They all wanted the gold rinse to match the mitre.' At this point the man in the box laughed so loudly that it set us both off and we could hardly act the rest of the sketch. Luckily I could walk upstage and pretend to get scissors and hair-spray, but Lance was stuck in the chair, in full view of the house, and he went through an agony of mirth.

I still laugh whenever I think of it. There was a terrible row afterwards and the stage manager came round and berated us. 'You ruined the performance by corpsing on stage. It's a disgrace.' At that point the stage-door man came in and announced the occupant of the box. In walked one of the greatest American exponents of Liszt, George Bolet. I'd heard him play in the film *Song Without End*. I was staggered that a concert pianist of his stature should stroll into my dressing-room and say he was a fan.

'I want to congratulate you on a wonderful show,' he said, and he sang our praises fulsomely. 'Gentlemen, it's a triumph!' he concluded.

The stage-manager sycophantically concurred. 'I was just telling Mr Williams, sir, what a wonderful performance it had been.'

Afterwards I said to the stage-manager, 'Well, that was a

fine *volte face*. You said at first we were disgraceful, but then you told George Bolet it was marvellous.'

'Ah, my dear,' he countered, 'the customer's always right.'

27 January

Health warnings appear on everything these days and I see in a letter to *The Times* today someone has written that, 'Since health warnings appear on cigarettes and people are now telling us we mustn't drink coffee because it contains caffeine, that tea contains tannin, and butter contains cholesterol, the government should print on our birth certificates, "Life is about dying".' Quite right.

The Times has got another piece about the dangers of alcohol. It's actually claimed that whisky kills more people than bullets. It's all quite ridiculous, because, as any child knows, bullets don't drink whisky.

At least it's an easy crossword today – no hazard to health there.

31 January

My confidante at the health food shop was in one of her didactic moods today.

'You'd be amazed at the ignorance of the general public,' she said. 'I had a customer in the other day who didn't even know that vinegar was sour wine.'

I said, 'I didn't know that myself.'

'There you are, and you'd call yourself a knowledgeable man, wouldn't you?'

'Well, ye. . . .'

'Exactly. Vinegar is a natural astringent. You might as well put after-shave on your salad. It shrinks the stomach.'

I shuddered. 'Then I shall certainly avoid it. I don't want to walk round with a shrunken stomach.'

I fled into the street grasping my wheat loaf and thinking for some extraordinary reason of Mahatma Gandhi.

Heard a lovely story at the Cosmo restaurant tonight. The owner said he'd overheard one mittel-European lady tell her friend she'd paid five-fifty to see *Dr Zhivago*.

The other woman exploded, 'Five-fifty! What is he, some sort of specialist?'

February

2 February

Got a letter today from the Jury Summoning Officer wanting me to report for the London Petty Sessions. I replied saying that I was an actor, that I frequently played the parts of judges and satirized them, and hardly thought I was suitable for jury service. Hope it works.

4 February

Last night I had to remove the eiderdown again. The weather really has become incredibly mild.

Postcard this morning from Gordon Jackson in Madeira saying it is full of English people and several Scots. One lady had bearded him in the corridor, saying, 'I know your face. I've watched if often enough on the telly,' to which Gordon made a suitably polite remark, whereupon she added, 'but it's nice to see you without turning the knob.' Gordon replied, 'Yes, madam, and considerably less painful,' and left a perplexed admirer as he swept on to his room.

Walked to Osteria Lariana and met Jeremy Swan who was my first director on *Jackanory*. He was in high spirits and told me about bumping into an old chum of his who'd been stage-managing a tour of the ballet, *A Midsummer Night's Dream*, starring Robert Helpmann. On one of their American dates there was no suitable theatre available and they performed in a floodlit sports arena, at night, with great success.

Robert Helpmann was allocated the umpire's dressing room, since this was the most commodious and they thought the star should have the best accommodation. When the stage-manager went round and called the half-hour, he received no answer from the umpire's dressing room, so he opened the door to check that the actor was present, and found Robert Helpmann standing on a chair, which was itself standing on a table, craning his face to the solitary lightbulb dangling from the ceiling, doing an elaborate green and gold eye make-up for his part as Oberon.

'Are you all right up there?' asked the stage manager in some alarm. Robert looked down and said, 'Oh yes, I'm fine. But heaven knows how these umpires manage.'

Such eccentric humour reminded me also of the actor I worked with at Birmingham Rep who always made every discussion come back to food in some way or another. He said to me once, 'I popped over to see the Redgraves and we had a strawberry on the lawn.' He made it sound like intercourse.

Freddie Treves once asked this same actor, 'Weren't you in the navy during the war?' He said he had been, and named the destroyer. Treves said, 'I remember that ship, she was sunk.' 'Yes,' said the actor, 'we were picked up by a French corvette and we had the most wonderful omlettes fines herbes on board.' All he could remember from the dire emergency was the quality of the cuisine!

Jeremy and I then fell to discussing touring and I told him I hated it. I don't like being out of my own place and continually in rooms in digs or in hotels. I don't like it at all. The last occasion was in '76 when I did a Feydeau farce called *Signed and Sealed*. We got to Newcastle and were playing to terrible business because a heat-wave struck England and anything that wasn't air-conditioned, wasn't patronised. We had a handful out front for the whole tour and it was truly lowering. One's morale sank round the ankles as one found about fourteen people sitting in those vast Northern theatres.

We got to the third act one night when the manager came into my dressing-room and said, 'I've written this speech for you to read at the end of the play.'

I said, 'I beg your pardon. We're doing a comedy. I'm not reading any speeches at the end of the play.'

'I don't think you've heard,' he said. 'It was on the news tonight. Dame Cyril Thorndike has died.'

'You mean Dame *Sibyl* Thorndike.'

'It was in this very theatre that she played *Candeeda*.'

'You mean *Candida*,' I countered.

'She played *Candeeda* in this very theatre, so we must mark the occasion and pay tribute to her from the stage at the end of the show.'

'I'm not paying any tributes to the dead from the stage after an attempt, pathetic though it may be with only fourteen people out front, to play a three-act comedy by Feydeau,' I told him. 'I'm not doing any sad chats at the end of that. It would be singularly inappropriate. We'll take the curtain, we'll take the applause. The pianist will play them out with a suitable little tinkle on the keys and then I'm going.'

'But you don't understand,' he said, 'This woman has *died*.'

'I've been on tour for five weeks,' I told him, 'and I've died every night, but no one's read a funeral oration over me.'

I told Jeremy this story and he said it was a shame I hadn't enjoyed the Feydeau. 'After all you had a great success with Charles Laurence's comedy, *My Fat Friend*. I've often wondered why you left it.'

'I had to leave,' I said. 'I had trouble with my colon.'

He laughed. 'I never bother with them. I just use a full stop.'

7 February

Yes, it *has* worked! Received a reply today from the Jury Summoning Officer saying, 'I agree with you about your unsuitability for jury service. I fear you would cause quite the wrong kind of levity in court.'

9 February

Extraordinary the letters one receives. I got one this morning saying,

> You don't seem to realize there's another world outside the glitter and tinsel of showbiz. Take off your blinkers, look around you at the ordinary people, the salt of the earth, people who do an honest day's work by the sweat of their labour, people who don't travel in taxis and drink champagne out of somebody's slipper, who scrape along unheralded, uncomplaining and unsung.
> Yours sincerely, Zsa Zsa Gabor.

Must be an impostor.

11 February

Am thinking about taking a holiday, even though last year's trip to Cyprus nearly finished me. Everyone had said Cyprus possessed a pleasant all-year-round climate, but I found only rain in February. The taxi from the airport to Limassol was raucous with pop music blaring from the car radio, and every time I complained the driver affected deafness. The hotel was still being constructed, and in the reception area there was a mass of rubble. The desk clerk said, 'We are enlarging the place, you see'. In the room, glass doors leading to the balcony were full of jagged cracks covered with hastily applied sticking-plaster. The porter said, 'It was the wrong thickness, we have ordered new glass'. The windows looked down upon a rain-soaked mud patch with cement-mixers and building material lying in a forlorn heap. 'It's like a junk yard!' cried Louie, my mother, whose holiday optimism had rapidly abated during the journey.

It reminded me of the backstage theatre conditions for Maggie Smith during the *Private Lives* run in New York. The dressing room was a shambles and Mags was sitting in the midst of peeling decay when the manager called to apologise: 'I am sorry about the state of the place, but the building is going to be demolished.' 'Lend me a pick-axe', suggested Maggie brightly, 'I'll give you a hand!'

I felt the same way about my Limassol hotel; everything was tatty, the rooms, the staff, and the food. After dinner on the first night we were offered one piece of stale cheddar. When the waiter asked if we required anything more, I shuddered involuntarily: 'No thank you! The cheese-board was overwhelming!'

Leaving Cyprus provided no relief; the journey back was a nightmare. The plane was held up for ages. Then everyone was made to leave the forward section. We were told that a government party was coming aboard, and that instead of going to London, the plane was being diverted to Paris. Eventually the President, ministers, and officials made a noisy entrance and we took off. Throughout the journey they were plied with drinks, food and attention, while the rest of us, hungry and thirsty, smouldered with resentful chagrin. I was glad to see the back of them at Orly airport where a red carpet was laid down and a band played while the President inspected a guard of honour which looked about as enthusiastic as we did. The aircraft waited endlessly on the tarmac because of haggling over the refuelling and when we finally got to London we'd been stuck in that plane for over ten hours! As we got off, the cabin crew had the gall to suggest that we should use their airline again and make another visit to their 'beautiful island'. I thought, 'not if I can help it. Aphrodite's home it may be, but my idea of an idyll it isn't.'

Also I had had to endure all that bogus bonhomie from fellow-travellers loquacious with duty-free liquor: 'Carry on Kenny!' 'Stop messin' about' and 'Speak for sixty seconds!' they chorussed. Comradeship is all very well, but undue familiarity can sour one – though on some occasions it can be very funny.

Kenneth Connor told me about one of the painters on the set during the shooting of *Trio* (the film from the story by Maugham). The overalled workman went up to the ageing writer who was sitting in a canvas chair watching a breathtaking scene, and whispered, 'You've got another winner there, Somerset!'

Perhaps there's something about filming that encourages the untoward. On another picture, starring an actress who was notorious for her Women's Lib injunctions to 'throw away the bra', an electrician told the star, 'Makes you look ten years younger – the breasts hanging down like that have taken all the wrinkles out of your face!'

17 February

Went to the Equity Council meeting. It's amazing how seriously some people take it. One councillor told me that when the referendum was on, someone told Marius

Goring that Edith Evans had just died. 'Oh dear', he said, 'I hope she filled in her ballot form.'

The meeting was taken up by the consequences of the Appeals Committee procedure and there was a lengthy motion asking for an independent enquiry. Someone suggested ACAS. Several councillors spoke of the waste of the Council's time and the motion was eventually defeated. When economic recession and this appalling climate combine to damage our business, why do we have to have these ludicrous wranglings over trivialities?

After the meeting, I spoke to Isabel Dean about the book she gave me by Professor Gowers, *Plain Words*. I love the bit where he goes on about the misuse of the plural and says that the English frequently fall into the error of saying 'the government *are* not doing enough for the plight of the country' instead of 'the government *is* not doing enough. . . .'. My favourite is the example he gives from *Hamlet*. 'It is true,' writes Gowers, 'that Ophelia says "There is pansies", but she was not herself at the time.'

18 February

Bumped into Maudie – Fun with a Frankfurter – Fittleworth in John Lewis's.

'I've just come back from a tour of the East,' she confided. 'I was with Korean Crackers, top-billing – Maudie Fittleworth – "Fun With A Frankfurter". Oh, my dear, it was a great success, but I had to cope with endless emergencies! When one of my frankfurters hit the fan in Seoul, I did a marvellous ad-lib about sliced salami. But really my stuff's wasted on foreigners.'

She was with a pale, languid young man whom she introduced as Adrian. 'Hello,' he said. 'We've already met.'

'I don't remember,' I replied.

'Yes, at the BBC, when you were in wardrobe for *Jackanory*.'

Then the penny dropped. 'Oh . . . yes,' I stammered. 'You look different.'

'Well, I had my wig then. Now I've had the transplant.'

I affected admiration for the sparse tufts sprouting on the scalp and Maudie swept us all into the cafeteria for tea.

'Adrian's trying to get the BBC interested in my act. He got me an interview with the titular heads there. I met them in the boardroom. I knew they were titular because they kept falling forward. I thought we might be boring them and I said, "Are we boring you?" but they said their teeth were full of lead fillings and that made them top-heavy.'

When Maudie went to powder her nose, I told Adrian, 'I take her stories with a pinch of salt. In fact you need more than a pinch, you need a lot.'

He said, 'Darling, you need Lot's wife.'

19 February

Went to a dreadful party. Spent the whole evening trying to avoid faces stuck far too close to me, all of them reeking of cold germs. Talking to one sneezing guest I found myself mentioning my love for Guercino and the man said, 'Perhaps you'd like to come to my home. I have a painting of his.' 'Not with your germs,' I thought, but out loud I said, 'Yes . . . it's the light, isn't it? The light is magical. You can see the influence of Caravaggio.' And then I fled.

When I got home, I helped myself to Andrews and Paracetamol, but I was still meandering about at 3 o'clock in the morning. I should never go to parties.

21 February

Still feeling groggy, went to the Cosmo with Michael and was disgusted to find him looking the picture of good health. 'No drink, that's why,' he explained. 'Only mineral water. Why don't you have some?'

'No thanks,' I said, 'I'm trying to give it up.'

During the meal the manager came over and talked about the problems of running a restaurant. 'When I was in charge of the Midland Hotel, you know, for British Rail in Manchester, some uniformed men arrived and collected the Bechstein concert grand. Only later did we find out that they were all dressed in stolen uniforms and that the piano had been pinched.'

Michael said, 'Well, I've heard of the lost chord, but that's ridiculous.'

23 February

Went to see Saul Radomsky about the set for *Entertaining Mr Sloane*. Discussed the costumes at length. His ideas are all very good. Got away by one.

In the afternoon there was a call for me to do *The Pyramid Game* on LWT on Friday, then a second call for me to go on Radio London with Lorraine Chase. Then Nick Spargo came on about doing the voices for the animated series *Willo-the-Wisp*. So it's all happening. I was right not to go away for a holiday – particularly as I start three weeks' rehearsal of *Sloane* at Hammersmith tomorrow.

24 February

Before rehearsals today I went to Radio London for the interview and phone-in with Lorraine. She handled it with great aplomb and gave me a lift afterwards. I thought how strange it was that such frail wrists could control the wheel of a very powerful motor-car.

I remember being on tour with Lorraine in a play called *The Undertaking* in Brighton. She raised quite a few eyebrows in the Royal Crescent Hotel when she demanded loudly in the foyer. 'You got a pail I can wash me 'air in?'

I said to her, going up in the lift, 'Why don't you use a shower?'

'I've got very long hair, and it's better in a pail,' she answered. Weird.

She suggested going for a stroll before the play that night and we went up to Rottingdean, where she teetered about on dangerously high-heeled, open-toed shoes, looking every inch a model, trying to cross the stony beach like a ballerina on points.

'You should wear sensible shoes,' I told her.

'I'm totally disorganised,' she said. 'I've just brought the things for the show.'

In the play she had to spend the first half lying on her back without moving. She was supposed to be an effigy and look wonderfully madonna-like. Lying stock-still on stage is bad enough, but when she came to rise, she had to lift herself effortlessly from the waist. She always did this with such consummate ease and grace that I realized the tremendous stamina and physical strength stored in that delicate, graceful frame.

27 February

Rehearsed all morning at Hammersmith then went on to LWT for *The Pyramid Game*. I worked with various contestants and talked to Joyce Blair and Julia MacKenzie, Dicky Davis and Lance Percival. It was really quite pleasant. Then we went down to the studio and sat waiting while other games were in progress. Eventually at nine o'clock, the head of light entertainment, David Bell, came down and said to me, 'Look we're not going to use you, because we've run out of contestants. It's a good job you're a pal and I know you. You can go home.'

So I left, feeling vaguely humiliated, but then reflected that since I was paid, it was an insult I could pleasantly swallow.

March

2 March

Went to BBC television and talked with Nigel Williams about the Arena programme on Joe Orton which will coincide with the opening of the play. He gave me lunch with his boss. They wanted to talk about some other aspect of Orton's life apart from playwriting. I told them that it would be a good thing to mention that he frequently wrote to the papers under the assumed name of Edna Wellthorpe.

I once went to Joe's flat in Noel Road and found it awash with cans of preserved fruit. Joe and his friend Kenneth Halliwell told me that they had written to Crosse and Blackwell complaining about the contents of a can they had purchased. They showed me a copy of their letter which said,

> Your blackberry fruit pie filling proved disastrous and my aunt Lydia is languishing on a day-bed, having been up half the night as a result of eating your dreadful product. You say on the label, glucomates have been added. Yes, and one wonders what else you've added to bring about this extraordinary malaise.
> Signed Edna Wellthorpe.

Within a week a reply was received:

> We were appalled to read about your aunt's condition and only hope that she is recovered. We can assure you this is most unusual. You must have got a bad batch and we will certainly see to it that you are provided with some new tins of blackberry fruit pie filling, which will, we hope, meet with your fullest approval.
> Cordially yours, etc. . . .

And they'd received masses of the stuff, enough to last for months and months.

The *Arena* producers thought this was a charming sidelight and I told them that it wasn't the only Edna Wellthorpe episode. Joe and Ken had also written to a vicar asking for the loan of his church hall to mount what was described as a defence of homosexuality entitled *Nelson Was A Nance*. As an amateur group of players, Edna explained, they hadn't the money to hire a theatre, but knowing that the Church took a tolerant and compassionate view of sexual deviance, she was sure that the vicar would give them the church hall free. The reverend gentleman replied:

> I'm afraid the letting of the church hall is not in my
> hands. It is a matter for the elders who meet
> half-yearly. In any case, I frankly don't feel that
> they would approve of any play which lampoons a
> national hero like Nelson. I can't help feeling that
> your efforts at enlightenment are not being
> directed towards the proper causes. There are
> many more worthy appeals with which you could
> identify in terms of Christian charity.
> Sincerely yours. . . .

They wrote back again, this time pretending that they were Edna's mother:

> Doubtless you've read in the paper about the
> demise of my daughter, Edna. In a cupboard
> under the stairs I found her voluminous
> correspondence on behalf of the amateur group
> which is attempting to mount their controversial
> play *Nelson Was A Nance*. As Edna's mother, I
> feel that I would like to carry on my daughter's
> wonderful work with these talented and devoted

people. Accordingly I wonder if you would reconsider your decision on letting the church hall.

They got a second reply from the vicar which read,

Dear Mrs Wellthorpe,
I was appalled to read of the death of your daughter. Alas, I did not see it in the local paper, I do not take it. But I am very sad to hear that she has passed on. On the other hand I can't help feeling that she got in with the wrong set.

Joe and Ken entered into another correspondence under the guise of Edna Wellthorpe, this time with the manager of the Ritz. The first letter read,

Dear Sir, I recently visited your hotel and was astonished at the opulent surroundings. I was accompanied by my friend, Mrs Sullivan. You'll remember her, she was the one in the fur coat. We took tea in your resplendent lounge, but unfortunately we discovered on arriving home that my brown, moroccan leather handbag was missing. Would you please arrange a search by your staff, because this is of deep sentimental value to me. Also, Mrs Sullivan left a pair of gloves made of sticky vegetable matter. The bag contained a Boots folder with snaps of Mrs Sullivan and me in risqué poses. You will naturally appreciate that neither of us wish such things to fall into the wrong hands.

The manager of the Ritz replied,

An exhaustive search by our staff has failed to uncover any moroccan leather handbag. But I am delighted to hear that you enjoyed your tea with us and assure you of our constant attention at all times.

'Edna' wrote back, saying,

I find it difficult to believe that such an obvious article has not been found. All enquiries from the other places we visited have revealed nothing. Are you sure some member of your staff has not secreted them somewhere and is furtively enjoying an unhealthy sexual gratification from looking at the foolish antics of two ladies of advanced years?

The Arena people liked the Wellthorpe stories and want me to use them in the programme – so Edna will be revealed on TV. Hope Joe and Ken won't mind her underwear being washed in public.

4 March

None of the actors know their lines yet! Saw Stanley Baxter later and told him about it. 'Don't rush them,' he said, 'or you'll provoke the actor's nightmare about forgetting the words. It's the thing of beginning with confidence, then going through that awful crisis thinking that you'll never be able to do it, and then coming back eventually to an assurance that you never thought you'd recapture. It's the old actor's syndrome.'

I hate mispronunciation. 'You don't say the word with a long o,' I told him. 'You don't say "epitome" with a long o, or "Penelope" with a long o, you say "epitome" and

"Penelop*e*", accentuating the final e because they are Greek derivatives. So you say "syndrom*e*".'

'Are you sure?'

'Yes. If you wish, you can consult the *Oxford English Dictionary*, but you will find that I am right.'

'Well, I've never said "syndrom*e*",' Stanley said, 'I've always said "syndr*o*me".'

'Well, you're wrong,' I told him. 'You know what Shaw said about ignorance: "Enlighten it".'

Then he showed me some snaps taken on his recent holiday. I said, 'Well, it looks enchanting, you must have had a lovely time.'

'Yes, I did,' he replied, 'I'd never done that part of Italy before. We left from Pisa, where they have a charming aerodromy.'

I retreated, hoist by my own petard.

6 *March*

Did a voice-over for an insecticide commercial this morning. Walked to the sound studios, tucked away behind all those stalls in Berwick Street. The producer said, 'We've worked together before. Do you remember?'

I didn't.

'Of course, you're looking wonderful,' I lied brilliantly. 'Is that your own hair?'

I was away in under ten minutes. As I departed, one of the stallholders who had seen me go in called out, 'Hardly worth getting up for, was it, Ken?' and I laughed gaily as I fled to Hammersmith.

At rehearsals today Barbara (Windsor) was surrounded by the TV cameras for the Arena programme. They wanted a close-up of the moment in the play when she takes the boy's trousers down – and they got it. He was dreadfully embarrassed. 'If I'd known, I'd have worn my other under-pants,' he said.

Barbara said, 'No, keep your best pair for Sunday.'

13 March

Went to the Greenwood Theatre which was endowed by a surgeon called Greenwood. Apparently his will stated, 'Build a theatre', so they erected one for actors instead of for doctors. It's a hateful place, the wind blows everywhere. The BBC use the Greenwood as a television theatre now. I was doing a chat with Barry Took about the *Round the Horne* series and sang a couple of the Rambling Sid songs on the show.

I said to Barry afterwards, 'I often found the preamble to those songs funnier than the lyrics themselves – lines like "We fell to chatting by the wayside over a rude meal of hedgehog pâté washed down with a simple, unpretentious bottle of parrafin rosé" are delightful, as is: "It is an old Sussex courting song and tells the story of a young swain, who stands beneath his loved one's bower. He's a very small swain, but then she's got a very low bower. It's the prevail-ing winds, you see." '

I said how sad it was that so much radio today consists of audience participation stuff, like phone-ins, which are shapeless and largely inarticulate, or else unscripted panel games. 'Where have all the writers like you and Marty Feldman gone?'

'To television and Hollywood,' said Barry. 'Radio is very much the poor relation these days. The visual shows get the big budgets and consequently much of the talent that was once going into sound is now exclusively reserved for the screen.'

I thought afterwards, he's right, but there are still things that can only be done on radio. Major Bloodknock pulling the lavatory chain and crying 'No more curried eggs for me!' would be impossible in any other medium.

14 March

Joan Sims rang. 'My mother's just died', she said, 'and the undertaker's bill says I get a ten per cent discount if I pay promptly. There's scant regard for the bereaved these days. And Southend Council have written an illiterate piece asking when the furniture in the house is to be disposed of. It's a bit much, you know.'

16 March

Still toying with the idea of a break after the play has opened. Talked to a woman at the travel agency. She mentioned a comparatively unspoilt resort on the island of Mykonos. 'It's very hot,' she said. 'You get masses of sun, marvellous food and it's a naturist's paradise. Everyone's nude; you can just let everything hang out. I had a marvellous fortnight there. Nobody wore a stitch of clothing. The freedom of the whole place is wonderful. The proprietor is a fine specimen of a man. His twenty children do all the catering and cleaning.'

'Twenty children?'

'Yes – that's nudism for you.'

'Nudism be blowed,' I said. 'He just never had time to dress.'

17 March

Had a phone call from Stanley Baxter. He asked. 'Have you ever had any publishers asking you to do a biography?'

I said, 'Yes.'

'So have I,' he replied, 'but it's a daunting prospect, isn't it? All those white sheets of paper. I'd go snow-blind.'

'Talking of books,' I said, 'I'm reading this absorbing volume on the Hapsburgs. I didn't realize how Elizabeth of Austria met her end.'

'Well, how?'

'She was going along the jetty to take the steamer across the lake at Geneva when a boy bumped into her, very rudely. She was quite unaware he had wounded her. She thought he was a hooligan. Only later did the blood start to appear on the bodice of her dress, and she realized that he had stabbed her with a very fine stiletto blade.'

'Yes – he obviously had the dead needle to her,' said Stanley.

'I don't know how you can say anything so horrid as that – you *are* callous.'

'That's right, just call me Maria,' he said and rang off.

I laughed in spite of the irreverence. Stanley's *bon mots* are always amusing. I needed cheering up after today's run-through.

18 March

First Night tonight. I never dreamed that when Joe gave me the inscribed copy of *Entertaining Mr Sloane* I would one day be directing the play. I took that copy to the Lyric recently and used it for the rehearsal. Weird to think that a present in '65 becomes the tool for my trade in '81.

Tube to the Lyric. Went round to see the cast to wish them well. An extraordinary thing happened backstage. I've been insistent about having a very large handle on the main door of the set. Day after day at rehearsals it hasn't been in evidence and I've continually cried, 'Where's my knob? I've been promised a big knob.' Tonight I got it. The stage management crew presented me with a wooden dildo in a specially made bag with their greetings embroidered on the material. I demurely declined. I said I'd rather take the wrapper, if it was all the same to them.

The performances were all fairly good. I saw Gerald Thomas in the foyer, who said that Barbara was marvellous. And Michael Anderson said he thought it was going beautifully. The gramophone failed unfortuantely — a speaker was defunct, which was infuriating. Altogether, though, it was as good as one can expect, though I fancy we shall get a lukewarm reception from the press.

19 March

No! A fabulous notice in *The Times*. 'Kenneth Williams has seized on the acting to make the play more insidious. His production has the honourable distinction of making such lives seem ordinary. Nothing seems bizarre. The production is splendid in its nasty normality.'

Am *very* pleased.

20 March

Went to the Lyric to congratulate the cast on their notices and saw Bob McKenzie in the foyer. He reminded me of the time we were all together in Tangiers with Joe Orton and the Reuters' correspondent, George Greave.

'Yes,' I said to Bob, 'George was a great chum of Joe's, though he didn't always relish Joe's hospitality. He once told me about a tea-party in Joe's flat in the rue de Mershaum. His friend, Richard, the masseur went with him. Joe had a huge cake on the table, a big brown one. George said "That's a nice cake." And Joe and Halliwell started giggling. "What are you laughing at?" George asked, "I just mentioned a cake, that's all." They started giggling again and said, "It's a hashish cake." George didn't believe them, but Richard had a bit and he seemed all right, so George decided to have a bit too. Then the whole room started reeling, and with his bulk, George has terrible trouble balancing at the best of times. He nearly fell off the chair. Richard got them a taxi. It was an awful job but he and Halliwell got George in eventually and he passed out. Only when he came to did he realize they'd been telling the truth: it *was* hashish.'

Bob McKenzie fell about at the thought of George Greave full of hashish being bundled into a taxi. I asked Bob if he had taken that flat in Judd Street which I had warned him against.

He told me, 'No. I'm very grateful for you telling me about that block. The noise would have been intolerable. Everyone seems to ignore the clause in the lease that says "All tenants shall be entitled to peace and quiet".'

'I know,' I said. 'I mentioned that clause to Danny La Rue when he was having trouble in his flat and he said, "Oh, I've got the piece, dear, but it's seldom quiet".'

22 March

Mags (Maggie Smith) phoned and came over. We went to Drone's for dinner.

She said Bev (Beverley Cross, her husband) was working

on a script. 'There are times when he needs solitude, because that's when an author wants to be alone and just concentrate on writing,' but she avowed that he was the best possible companion. 'I've been living out of a suitcase for years and I still find it irksome not to have my own place and roots, but Bev copes with a nomadic existence with perfect equanimity. He can be at home anywhere.'

'Yes,' I said. 'When we were in Crete we went to the monastery at Topolu where Makarios spent his novitiate, and where Bev said we could spend the night. An orthodox monk was showing us the mosaics that had been whitewashed by the Turks and then carefully restored to their former splendour. He told us about the Turkish occupation and about how everything had to be renovated. I was affecting great interest when I noticed Beverley sidling away. I said to him when we got to the corridor, "You should have looked more interested, that man was explaining everything."

He said, "No thank you, I saw the lice in his beard."

"How awful," I said, "I wish you'd never mentioned that. I feel terrible now" – and was sure that I was itching.

When we got out of the long corridor to the refectory, two of the monks told us, "It is customary for us to offer you the hospitality of the monastery and guests can sleep overnight since the journey to Sitia is so long. We offer you these very simple cells, where straw pallets are provided."

After the lice I wasn't interested in straw pallets. I was dying to get out. "No, we're going on," I said. They told me that it was going to take a long time to reach Sitia, but I said, "I don't care if it takes all night and the following day, I'm leaving."

They had to lower a drawbridge. It was like a medieval castle. This Greek boy, Stavros, who was driving us, got us to Sitia, after driving half the night, and said, "There is no place here, you have to ask the headman of the village to provide something." We enquired and eventually rooms were found. I had one with a jug and bowl in the corner, but although the conditions were pretty crude, I said to Beverley that no matter how primitive, anything would be better than that flea-ridden monastery.

At the end of our time in Sitia we were entertained by the headman. During the meal, I said to an English girl who was a graduate of Athens University and supposed to speak Greek, "I would like to say a little something at the end, in Greek, in response to my hosts."

"What do you want to say?" she asked.

"Well, something like 'I love the people of Greece'."

"Well you say *Agapo tous anthropous tis Elladas*."

So I learnt that and when my turn came, I got up at the table and said, "I have learned a Greek phrase and I would like to say to you all tonight, with deep sincerity, *Agapo tous anthropous tis Elladas*." They all started laughing. I laughed, too, because I thought that's what you were supposed to do. When I came out, I said to Stavros, "Why did they all laugh when I said *Agapo tous anthropous tis Elladas*?"

He said, "It means 'I love the men of Greece'."

'Oh no! I meant the *people*."

'Well, what you said applied only to the men," said Stavros. "They thought you were being very bold".'

Mags laughed and said 'It only goes to show Pope knew it all: "A little learning . . ." '

25 March

In the dentist's waiting-room today there was a weird old man wearing rubber wading boots and two sou'westers. He looked like a deep-sea fisherman about to brave the poop-deck. Seeing me eye his apparel, he suddenly spoke: 'London could be flooded at any minute.'

41

Well, I thought, we could be run over at any minute, but I'm not walking round with splints and a stretcher. So I just nodded and affected interest in a tattered copy of *Country Life*.

28 March

Watched the *Parkinson* show tonight. There were some good moments, but nothing tops Robert Mitchum's reply when Michael said, 'With your famous face, don't you find you can't go anywhere without being recognized?'

He half opened his eyes and drawled, 'No, it's no problem. I often slip out of the Dorchester in drag.'

He spoke so solemnly that Michael was nodding assent and looking quite serious right up to the last word.

Stanley Baxter once described to me how he was getting into his open car, which was parked in a side street, and was just putting it into gear, when a man passing by stopped, with his arm outstretched and shouted, 'Wait a minute. I know that face. What's your name? No, it's on the tip of my tongue. No, no, don't tell me. I'll get it in a minute. Don't tell me . . . don't tell me. . . .' Stanley said shortly, 'I won't,' and drove off, leaving the man in a haze of complexity and carbon monoxide. But then he had the advantage of mobility.

I had no such luck in Bordeaux. The aircraft had put down there in an emergency. In fact an engine fell off, and we made it to Bordeaux on just one, which is why some Frenchman's greenhouse is heated by a turbo-jet at the expense of the English taxpayer. In Bordeaux we were told to stay in the transit lounge, where we had to await the arrival of a relief plane.

In voices that could be heard on the tarmac, two burly

drunks asked loudly, 'Are you that poof on the telly?' stabbing me in the chest with their forefingers.

I could vanish nowhere; we had orders not to leave the lounge and anyway I was pinned against the wall. I had no option but to nod assent and repeat the rude formula, 'Yes, I'm the poof on the telly.' They were considerably bigger than I was, I'm afraid of fisticuffs and discretion is the better part of valour. Not only that, it's also an effective way to avoid getting your face bashed in.

When the relief plane eventually did arrive, the captain told us to board it and I said, 'I'd be careful if I were you. There are two drunks here, both very aggressive, and I wouldn't take them on the aircraft.'

'I know your face,' he said disdainfully. 'You're an actor, aren't you? Just stick to being funny and let me fly the aeroplane, will you?'

'I'm sorry I spoke,' I said, crushed once more.

As we were winding our way across the tarmac in the hot sun, the two drunks fell over. One split his head open and the other one fell on top of him. As a result, we all had to troop back to the departure lounge and wait until the French police arrived to take them away. We found out that, after they had been hospitalized, they were put into prison for disturbing the peace.

Eventually we took off without them. When we were airborne, and presumably with the co-pilot at the controls, the captain came along and admitted he should have taken my advice. BEA, as it then was, had had to pay for both their medical treatment and their accommodation in the French gaol. 'I'm sorry I didn't listen to what you said,' he added.

'Well, I don't want to crow,' I told him, 'but you really should have taken notice.'

'Yes,' he said, 'but after all, actors know nothing about the hazards of flying.'

I replied very grandly, 'On the contrary, I practically lost my leg in the flying circus I was in.'

He looked at me with renewed respect and said, 'I'm sorry. I didn't realize you were one of us.'

I beamed, but failed to mention that the aerial sorties I'd referred to were with Kirby's Flying Ballet in *Peter Pan*.

April

1 April

Received an appeal through the post asking for contributions to a theatrical museum. I mentioned it to my friend Paul Richardson, whom I met in Marks and Spencer this morning. 'Who wants to pay to see Sarah Bernhardt's ear-trumpet', I asked, 'or a lock of Sarah Siddons's hair? I think theatrical museums are silly.'

Paul assented. 'An American told me the cult for performers' mementoes is booming in the States. Elvis Presley's bric-à-brac sells for vast sums of money. People will do anything to get hold of a set of Rudolph Valentino's dentures.'

'Oh yes, it's reached ridiculous proportions. They've even got the actual pair of tights worn by Barrymore as Hamlet. He wouldn't have them laundered, because he thought it was bad luck. They're under glass.'

Paul shuddered. 'After all those performances, I should think they'd need to be.'

3 April

Stanley Baxter took me to Osteria Lariana. 'I do like this place,' he said, 'because it's so empty. I can't stand people staring at me.' But Giovanni, the manager, said, 'Yes, you may like it empty, but it is no good for us.' Like all performers, he wants it packeroo.

Stanley went into quite a diatribe about the bureaucratic tyrannies that multiply and stifle creative stimulus. 'You're preaching to the convered,' I said. 'I have screamed about the parasitic nature of bureaucracy for years. The Byzantine empire did not sink because of decadence. It sank under the weight of red-tape. As Parkinson says, "If there is a way to delay an important decision, the good bureaucracy, public or private, will find it".'

Stanley said, 'Did he say that on his chat-show? It's very fluent for an ad-lib.'

'No, it was J. Northcote.'

'Oh,' said Stanley, 'I was only taking the Michael.'

4 April

Woke up this morning still obsessed with last night's discussion on the bureaucracy that affects all government. I thought to myself, 'What *is* the nature of English government.'

There is something ludicrous about our entire system of government. You take a semi-literate group who manage to get their names onto the electoral roll and you ask them to put a cross against the name of the candidate they choose to represent them in the House of Commons. What decides them in this choice? Is it the organizing ability of this aspirant to office? Is it his religious belief or his philosophical attitude? His feeling for humanity? His sense of compassion? No, of course not. Indeed, if you mentioned such qualities to people at the polling stations, they'd think you were some sort of crank. Their choice is guided by two things: the party of the candidate, and the persona of the candidate, or rather the public persona of the candidate, since Emerson and less kind people have pointed out that a man has as many personalities as he has friends. But the all-important thing is party, and sometimes even the dullest creature is successful where party apparatus works most smoothly. Whole areas in London seem to remain consistent to their party attitudes: you find that Tower Hamlets always return a Labour MP, Westminster a Conservative, and so on. The Tower Hamlets remain wretched and miserable, while Westminster gets classier and classier.

After the voting process, the winning party leader chooses a cabinet. This is done in much the same haphazard fashion as the ballot system. A man is made Minister of Agriculture and Fisheries who has probably never seen a fish in his life, and who wouldn't know a rod from a pole or a perch. Someone obviously ill qualifies as Minister of Health and an inarticulate who can't string enough words together to form a sentence is made Minister for Education. You have a Chancellor in the upper house who sits on the woolsack, because wool once symbolized the wealth of England. Today he ought to be sitting on an oil-drum.

These people all make noises and issue cliché-ridden statements about their intentions, but after a few weeks in office, everyone begins to realize that it is all depressingly similar to the time before. The system goes on inexorably, year in year out. Like Big Ben it's cracked, but it still tells you the time; an increasingly myopic electorate will soon have to be taken up the tower and made to feel the hands before they actually believe it.

6 April

Went to the BBC to see Helen Fry about the programme we're doing – 'It Makes Me Laugh'. I noticed how the occupants of a lift are inhibited during an ascent. Nobody speaks; everyone seems to be self-consciously mute. In the office, Helen, who is Head of Archives, played a recording of Yeats reading 'The Lake Isle of Innisfree', which apparently was inspired by his walking along the Strand and seeing a fountain with celluloid balls playing in it. This seems a far cry from the inspiration of the place itself.

The recording was very bad. I told Helen that the very idea of authors reading their own stuff is really an illusion, because the professional is much better qualified for the task. I had an argument recently with someone who had been listening to a poetry programme. When I had complained that the reader's delivery was so bad that it came between me and the meaning, he said, in tones of near-reverence, 'But that was the *author*', as though it was the ultimate criterion for judging the proper way to deliver a poem. 'Take that to its logical conclusion,' I said, 'and we'll have playwrights reading their own works and wondering why the theatres are empty.'

Helen then found the excerpt for which I'd asked: 'Frankie Howerd at the Establishment'. This is a marvellous recording. The material Frankie used is very funny and dwells at one point on a fantasy about his visiting Chequers to see the then Prime Minister, Harold Macmillan. There are some good lines: 'I went down on my bike, but couldn't get any answer. Mind you, I knew they were in there and I called out, "Dorothy, Dorothy, it's Frankie". There wasn't any reply and it was very difficult holding a conversation through the letter-box.'

I'd been present when the original recording was made and on the tape I could hear myself laughing. At one point Frankie pointed at me and said (it's on the disc) 'That's quite a spectacle, isn't it, one comedian laughing at another? I bet he'll pinch the material later on.' His prediction was correct.

'That's just what I'm doing for this programme,' I said to Helen as we ironed out the rest of the items we'd be using.

Made my way back to the lift and thought again about the way they discourage conversation. I was reminded of Ted Ray's story about the sadistic lift-boy in the Empire State Building, who took his lift to the sixtieth floor at such a speed that one of the women passengers was on the floor by the time it reached its destination. He leaned over and asked, 'You all right, lady?'

She staggered to her feet saying, 'Yes, I always wear my corsets round my ankles.'

7 April

Had a surprising call this morning from an old friend, Dennis Goacher, whom I haven't seen for years. He's over here from Greece and said he'd be in the British Museum reading room until lunch-time, and would I meet him at the gate. So I went along and we ate at a Greek restaurant nearby and revived many memories.

'I always connect this area with you,' I said, 'because you had that flat in Coptic Street and we used to have those hilarious dinners with Johnny Vere. Do you remember him telling us about the period when he was secretary to Edward Knoblock?'

'Yes,' said Dennis, 'it's curious how little Knoblock's remembered today. After all, everyone's familiar with Arnold Bennett, with whom he collaborated on the play *Milestones*, and yet Edward's name has dropped out of the public memory.'

'That's true,' I replied, 'and when he did enjoy a sort of resurgence it was thanks to *Kismet*, which was the musical based on his play. Johnny Vere said that, after Edward's death, he went through a very bad financial period. When *Kismet* was mounted at the Stoll Theatre, Johnny went along. He could see Gertrude Knoblock queening it in the royal box, so he went up to her and said, "Look Gertrude, I was your brother's secretary for many years. I slaved on his behalf and put up with all his idiosyncracies. I've been through a very bad patch, and you must be coining it in with the royalties from this show. What about you providing me with a little something, because I'm reduced to very near penury." She turned to Johnny very regally and said, "I will have a word with the administrators of the estate and see what can be done for you", as though she was handing out welfare. Johnny felt like somebody queueing up for the Silver Lady on the Embankment to get a cup of hot soup.

After a week he got a letter saying they were going to give him some shares that Edward had held for many years. Gertrude felt sure that Edward would have liked the dividends to accrue to Johnny. Since he was drawing the dole at the time, he was delighted. He had been reduced to taking two old Greek heads into a dreadful antique shop in the King's Road to try to flog them. As he was deeply fond of his Greek heads he was looking forward to this windfall from the shares. You can imagine his chagrin when he got twopence-halfpenny. The dividends were a joke because the shares were all in hooks and eyes, and of course zip fasteners had come in and completely ruined the market.'

10 April

Had a letter this morning asking for poetic guidance. The correspondent wanted to know the origin of 'Laugh and the world laughs with you'. I wrote back saying, 'I am delighted to be able to enlighten you, "Laugh and the world laughs with you" was written by Ella Wheeler Wilcox.'

As a matter of fact it had come as a bit of a surprise to me when I discovered it. I'd always thought that 'Laugh and the world laughs with you' was simply an old adage. I'd no idea it was part of her long poem *Solitude*, until I came upon the book *Evergreen Verse*.

After replying to the letter, I fell to thinking that an awful lot of exhortations to cheerfulness are frequently being addressed to us and I thought it would be a good idea to write one myself:

> If you can smile in the midst of pain
> And laugh at the cares of mankind,
> You're out of the mire,
> You're out of the rain,
> And you're probably out of your mind.

Went to bed feeling quite satisfied. Today a poet, tomorrow the Laureate.

12 April

Watched a television documentary about Alger Hiss tonight. One of the most telling moments in the Senate Committee hearing came when he prefaced his answer with a verbal conceit: 'I hate to disappoint you, Senator –'. 'You've already done that, Mister Hiss', interrupted Mundt wearily, and the ensuing laughter ruined Alger's reply. One saw the damage which ornament had caused. A direct response would not have provoked the witticism; but the speaker chose to be indirect, to decorate his speech with an attempted irony which backfired upon himself.

In grave matters levity is seldom effective unless you have the floor to yourself. In the end I think it comes back to sophistication. I remember Robert Bolt remarking upon the unsatisfactory nature of the dictionary definition of sophistication. Tracing its ancestry from the school of sophists was all very well, he said, but the modern sense of the word implied fluency, worldliness, and self-awareness. I think he was right. Every time self-awareness is lacking there is potential disaster. I'm always slightly shocked to see the evidence of this in any public event.

Watching a prize-giving occasion on television the other night, I marvelled at the number of actors mounting the dais to receive their awards, then making disavowals of the implied merit. One heard that 'they didn't really deserve it', and that those who *did* hadn't been recognized, that it was really the author, or the director, or the rest of the cast who should have been singled out. If one actually believed all that they said, we should have seen set-builders, make-up girls, stage-hands and costume-designers receiving the honours. Perhaps the odd tea-lady as well. Indeed, after listening to some of the winners, I fancy the tea-lady would have been more diverting. Having agreed to accept an award, it seems only proper to accept it gracefully. If it's given for serious work, the thanks should be serious. If it's for comedy, the thanks may contain a comic element, but both acceptances should acknowledge the giver and receiver in earnest exchange. Anything else invalidates the purpose of the occasion, and the value of the award.

Thank heavens not all actors are loath to trumpet their talents. When the elderly Ernest Thesiger, laden with parcels, had one foot on the bus and it suddenly started and began dragging him along, he called out to the conductor: 'Stop! You're killing a genius!' London Transport bowed to his exhortation and he was saved by the bell.

14 April

For no apparent reason, I was bearded by a girl in Bedford Square today who said, 'I've just been failed for RADA. It's another of a whole series of blows I've had to endure.'

I tried to cheer her up by telling her something of Joan Sims's appalling experience at RADA. She had won the Mabel Temelly Award for Grace and Charm of Movement. Joan told me, 'I had to mount a podium to receive it from Margaret Leighton.'

Full of curiosity I asked, 'What *was* the Mabel Temelly Award?'

'It was a cheque,' Joan said, 'presented by Margaret Leighton.'

'But, how much?' I asked.

She replied, 'Ten pounds'.

Kenneth Connor, who overheard this, said drily, 'You're on the same daily rate today'.

I told the girl this story in an effort to help her see what the business was really like. It made me think, too, of the occasion in the restaurant at Pinewood when Laurence Olivier came over and talked to us. He was down there playing Wellington in *Lady Caroline Lamb*.

'Don't these Carry On films pay you any money?' he asked. 'You all seem rather poor.'

Joan Sims replied, 'No, Larry – twopence-halfpenny. We're on twopence-halfpenny. It's appalling money.'

'Well, I was curious,' he said, 'because as I was coming down the Pinewood road this morning I saw this pathetic figure in an old mac, with two brown paper carrier bags struggling along the road, and I was sure I knew him. So I lowered the window and called out, "Isn't it Charles, Chalres Hawtrey?" and the figure looked up and said, "Oh yes, Sir Laurence." So I said, "Come in and I'll give you a lift." He told me he struggles along that road every day, getting the tube from Uxbridge, to film the Carry On pictures, which must make a lot of money. Surely they'd provide a motor-car for him?'

Joan said, 'No, we get no transport whatsoever. They won't pay a halfpenny for any extra comforts.'

And Barbara Windsor said, 'You've no idea what they put us through. We're filming in an orchard at the moment. It's a holiday sequence. We're supposed to be enjoying ourselves doing knees-ups and my feet were sinking into mud. It's the middle of winter and yet they're pretending we're all filming in the summer and they've got these men going round spraying green paint on the trees where the leaves have gone brown, because they won't film in the summer 'cos it costs too much.'

Larry departed saying he felt we all deserved something better and I commented afterwards, 'He'd never put up with Carry On conditions.'

'Oh,' said Joan, 'I'd wondered why they never cast him. . . .'

15 April

Spoke at a charity dinner tonight. It was death. I was stuck next to this lady who said, 'I treat my servants as equals', and she spoke *at* me the whole time, often with her mouth full. Ugh.

When I got up to talk I felt utterly doomed. The burden of my speech was the comical aspect of suffering. I pointed out to them that, unbeknown to the world at large, Idi Amin was in a London clinic incognito for the haemorrhoidal operation, and I added, 'They had to roll him in flour to find out where his arse is.' This was greeted with an embarrassed titter, so I quickly wound up with a line about my army medical, where I was paraded in embarrassing nakedness before three doctors sitting at trestle tables in the drill hall at Duke Street. One cried out irately, 'For heaven's sake, man, pull your stomach round to the front.' I had my back to him at the time. That occasioned enough laughter to allow me to regain my seat without losing face.

Afterwards I took my miserable little ticket to the cloak-room to collect my overcoat and stood in a queue of other men on a similar mission. Waiting there, I couldn't help overhearing one say, 'What did you think of the speakers?'

'Yes, all right,' said his friend, 'very good.'

'And what about that Kenneth Williams fellow?'

'Oh, a disaster.'

Whereupon I grabbed my coat and made a dash for the door. The commissionaire offered to call me a taxi, but I was so anxious to avoid my nemesis that I declined and blithely stepped out into the most crushing downpour of rain. I wandered up Sussex Gardens thinking how ludicrous it is to go these affairs, make a fool of yourself in public and then get soaked for your pains with no kind of remuneration.

18 April

Went to Stanley's house and Moira, his wife, said, 'We've got Kushi from Japan as our au pair boy. He's at London University and wants to improve his English.

'Au pair *boy*? What does he do for you?'

'Flower arranging, he does beautiful flower arranging. You'll meet him,' Stanley said. 'He'll come down in a minute. He does a lot of incense burning and obeisance at night.'

When Kushi came into the room he was carrying a tray with both coffee and tea. There were the usual introductions. Then he came to me and said, 'You like honourable cup of tea from honourable teapot?'

'Don't be absurd, Kushi'. I replied. 'A teapot is neither honourable nor dishonourable. It's earthenware. And when you have reached my age, you will realize the foolishness of these ridiculous phrases.'

'When I leach your age,' replied Kushi, 'I hope I no longer here.'

'How rude!' I exclaimed.

'It's your own fault,' said Stanley, 'you provoked him. It's a perfectly acceptable Japanese custom to refer to the pot as honourable. It was your own fault entirely.'

But I still felt very put out.

19 April

Saw Gordon today and he told me about getting the OBE while he was abroad. 'Somebody rang from the embassy to inform me confidentially that I was to receive the Order of the British Empire. I was quite taken aback. I didn't know we still had an empire. Anyway, I don't know what all the fuss is about. I put an X on the form for no publicity.'

'Oh I love any publicity that's to do with Buckingham Palace,' I said.

'You've been to the Palace?'

'Yes, they have this concert every year where the Queen entertains various members of the armed forces. They asked me once if I would like to take part and I said I would be honoured. On the day I hailed a taxi, and said "Buckingham Palace please".

"Eh? What did you say, guv?" asked the driver.

"Buckingham Palace," I repeated.

"Is that an hotel?"

"No – the Palace. . . ."

"The real thing, I've never been there."

"That makes two of us," I said.

We had to stop at the gates and a policeman poked his head in and asked who I was. I produced my pasteboard invitation and he said, "Oh, it's you. Go straight in, under the arch, round the back and they'll be waiting." I got inside and went into an ante-room where I was introduced to the others. There was a singer, a conjuror and the compère was Terry Wogan.

We were to perform in a large marquee in the grounds. It was very hot and the canvas retained the heat so that the sweat was pouring off us by the time we eventually performed. A tiny stage had been erected with little fairy lights all round it. Wogan went up to the microphone in the centre of the stage and started to speak, whereupon there was a terrible bang and all the lights went out. A lieutenant-commander appeared and announced, "Ladies and gentlemen, the main fuse to the Palace has blown and I must return to my ship," which I thought was rather odd.

Wogan said into the microphone, "Can you hear me?" at which they all shouted back "No". With amazing resource he said, "Then how did you manage to reply?" Thereafter we did without amplification. First on were a soprano and a baritone singing 'One Day When We Were Young' very beautifully. Next was a conjuror who produced an eagle owl from out of a pocket handkerchief with such amazing dexterity that I began to feel quite nervous.

They were all rather good. When my turn came, I was suddenly very worried because it had been made clear to me that everything we said "in the grounds of the Palace" had to be in the best possible taste. I had one line – "This girl was so thin that she looked like a do-it-yourself famine," – which I thought might be mistaken for an unkind reference to the anorexic. As it was, it got a good laugh, but the one that came next – "Even to have a shower, she has to keep moving" – got absolutely no response.

At the end of the show we came off drenched in perspiration, and I said to the equerry, "I could do with a very large gin and tonic". Came the reply, delivered with absolute flatness, "There is only beer, I'm afraid." And small beer it was, too.

20 April

Easter Monday.
Reading the Confucian lines: 'Nothing is more obvious than that which a man attempts to conceal; nothing more outwardly visible than the secrets of the heart', I realize their import but baulk at the use of the last word. Curious how men always attribute noesis to this organ. The same sentiment is expressed in Pascal's line: 'The heart has its reasons'. Hippocrates was right to insist that from the brain and the brain alone arises all our thoughts, our feelings, and our affections. The heart is a pump and because messages from the head determine the rate, its role in human activity becomes confusing for some. Romantics focus upon it as the repository of the affections and lines like 'I give you my heart' occur in love lyrics a-plenty. It's always the heart that is offered, never liver or kidneys, though donor cards are on the increase.

Philosophy is littered with labels which have been in and out of vogue depending on the latest persuasion. Because men sometimes choose to act badly, they often justify the consequences as 'instinctive behaviour', 'emotional reaction', 'intuitive response' and so on. Desire is masked as 'natural need', and modern medicine, with its psychological explanations of diminished responsibility, erodes the concept of praise and blame. The Confucian truth remains valid: 'Nothing is more obvious than that which a man attempts to conceal', and nowhere is it more evident than in acting. That is why the best performance is measured by its degree of vulnerability. The more we are shown, the more we respond. Technique is a Greek word for a bag of tools, and a good actor leaves you unaware of just how many he is using. Commenting on the vocal dexterity of one actor, I said to Stanley Baxter, 'He can create emotional effects that literally soar and hover on a stage. There are times when an actor is like a dragon-fly!'

'Certainly a fly,' he retorted, 'with its drag on.'

May

SELF-PORTRAIT
FRANK BARBER

GUIDE TO
NATIONAL
GALLERY

1 May

Got a challenging missive through the post this morning from a fan who finds it offensive that I am only, apparently, interested in light entertainment. She asks, 'Why don't you do something more substantial or serious on the box? Why this endless proliferation of games? We're always seeing you on *Give Us A Clue* or *Looks Familiar*, which don't really test your acting ability.' She also pointed out that the public are often used just as victims in these frivolous television shows. 'Surely you,' she concludes, 'with your firmly held convictions, deplore this tendency in modern life? Your sincerely, Freda Fuggle.'

I replied at length:

> Whether it's in the fiction of pantomime, or the horror of Northern Ireland, we see that cruelty and malice are inherent in human nature. Life and literature are pervaded by it. Moreover, the hurt itself attracts people, in deeds, as well as in words; hence the large audience for boxing matches, where crowds sit avidly watching blow after blow rained upon some unfortunate victim for no other gratification than their own vicarious pleasure. It is extraordinary to hear a commentator saying, 'He's opened that cut over the eye again!' seeming to praise what any self-respecting oculist would condemn. As far as I'm concerned, all trials of strength for public entertainment are as repugnant and distasteful as dirty fingernails on a pastrycook, but the miner whose shoulders sustain rotting pit-props while his fellows are rescued, arouses our admiration and elevates our sense of humanity, because his strength is used for a noble purpose and the example is uplifting to us

all. Every age, according to its spiritual resources, seeks to amplify its aspirations, and in our own poverty-stricken times our ambitions appear pitiful indeed. The modern world delights as much in the spectacle of the ignorant as the Romans did in watching gladiatorial combat.

Without the standards outside himself (which only religion provides) man's own standards are gradually eroded. He eventually arrives at the point where he no longer questions the public baiting of his fellow creatures. He sits and watches men and women misused and degraded in futile television 'games' which offer money or goods as Pyrrhic rewards for acting as amateur stooges in spuriously staged events. When one such embarrassment was held in America, they asked a foolish young lady: 'What is the difference between a fly and a wasp?' and she replied painfully, 'I don't know: I've never undone a wasp.' Apparently the audience responded with gales of laughter. The mirror image in a looking-glass world. But even this latter, with its curious significance for Mr Dodgson, is only possible because of values. To have something going backwards is only significant if it also moves forwards. The lie can exist only where there is truth. Philosophy and semantics give endless interpretations of truth.

Some people confuse truth with sincerity. Others fervently affirm that it 'will out' (whatever that may mean), others insist that it will set you free and a surgeon once told me that it was 'a pandora's box, only visible when the patient is cut open.' Unless you are a child, or very old, truth gets more and more like a will-o'-the-wisp. You can only find it in marshland, and bogs are not easy to negotiate. Still, Boadecia managed to find her way through some of the most treacherous in the fens, and cope with a horse and chariot as well, so it's not entirely hopeless, and if you think that will-o'-the-wisps aren't worth pursuing, just pause and remember that they can end up as domestic gas, keeping you warm and providing a boiling kettle for that lovely cup of tea. Used rightly, gas is beneficial, used wrongly it can blow up in your face. Truth is much the same.

I signed it 'Yours very sincerely, Maudie Fittleworth (Temporary Secretary to Kenneth Williams)' and put Maudie's address beneath. I reckon that if she can cope with the frankfurters she can cope with Freda Fuggle.

3 May

Went to Teddington to do *Give Us A Clue*. Louie came with Michael to watch it and at supper afterwards she told us about how she and Nelly Trigger were on the bus to her old-time dance club, and Nelly told her that she was getting rid of her old kitchen range and installing a tiled fireplace, so that it would be a kitchen-cum-dining-room. Louie asked what firebrick she would be using and Nelly told her 'a fourteen inch'. 'That's not enough,' said Louie. 'For that size room you'll need a sixteen inch.' The conductor interrupted saying, 'I can give you a sixteen inch,' and there was much ribald laughter from the other passengers on the bus.

Nelly reproved Louie. 'You shouldn't laugh at those sort of jokes, because men like that can get you up an alley and rape you.'

'Don't be silly, Nelly,' laughed Louie. 'He's not allowed to leave his bus!'

Obviously she considered London Transport to be entirely synonymous with virtue.

5 May

Found myself talking to Neil McCarthy, one of the actors in *Mr Sloane*, about staying in digs and he asked if I'd ever known a Mrs McKay.

'The one who said "Don't leave the chamberpot under the bed for the steam rises and rusts the springs"?'

'That's right,' said Neil. 'You know she's been the victim of urban renewal. The other day she told me, "The borough council are demolishing all the houses in this street. But we're getting communal compensation and I'll use that as cholesterol for another house. The bank will accept that, won't they?" "Certainly," I said. "They know what side their bread's buttered." '

6 May

I went to the BBC to collect Noël Coward's *Spangled Unicorn* and G. K. Chesterton's *Napoleon of Notting Hill*, which Helen Fry's secretary has got from the BBC library for the programme 'It Makes Me Laugh'. I'm going to read some of the best bits.

From the *Spangled Unicorn* I shall use Coward's Janet Urdler poem. 'Very little is known about Janet Urdler,' he writes 'but she seems to have spent most of her early years in the West Country. All she remembers is being taken for a ride by her aunt on a bullock cart through Dawlish.' Coward's happy combination of paradoxical sounds always make his work so diverting.

From the Chesterton I'm using Auberon's wonderfully dotty speech:

> In a hollow of the grey-green hills of rainy Ireland, lived an old, old woman, whose uncle was always Cambridge at the Boat Race. But in her grey-green hollow, she knew nothing of this: she didn't know there was a Boat Race. Also she did not know that she had an uncle. She had heard of nobody at all, except of George the First, of whom she had heard (I know not why), and in whose historical memory she put her simple trust. And by and by, in God's good time, it was discovered that this uncle of hers was not really her uncle, and they came and told her so. She smiled through her tears and said only, 'Virtue is its own reward'.

8 May

To the National Gallery today. Stomped through all the rooms, ignoring even my beloved Van Dycks, pausing only to gaze at the Guercino *Doubting Thomas*. They've inscribed it, 'The Incredulity of Thomas', which I find unnecessarily pompous. When I look at it, I am conscious of many things, but especially the strength, generosity and compassion of Guercino's Jesus.

When I was in Birmingham for the *Ad Lib* radio programme, I found two of Guercino's canvases in the City gallery. It was there that one of the attendants ruined my reverie. 'Guercino is really a nickname, you know. It means squint-eyed. His real name was Francesco Barbieri.'

Poor chap. The Italian version sounded much better than Frank Barber. As Miss Agatha Christie has amusingly observed, an opera by Joe Green wouldn't sound half so grand as one by Giuseppe Verdi. Once when I was introduced to a Spaniard called José Moreno, I said, 'In English you'd be known as Joe Brown.' 'Please don't call me Joe Brown,' he winced, as though the translation was some sort of abuse.

It's extraordinary how sensitive some people are about their names. Clement Freud won't tolerate being called Clem and says that if it must be shortened, make it Clay.

On the telephone people often call me Ken or Kenny, as well as Kenneth. I don't mind how matey they get as long as they do call.

13 May

Went to Dunne's today and bought a lounge-suit. I was amazed by the man there, who kept saying, 'For myself, I think that looks very good. I wouldn't take it up at all. For myself, I think that looks very nice.'

'But the sleeve is too long,' I said. 'You can't see any cuff.'

To which he replied, 'How many people bother with cuffs today?' as if I was living in the past. 'For myself, I would leave it as it is. That's what I would do if it was me.'

'But it's not you,' I cried, 'it's me.'

'Ah, yes, of course, you've got to wear it. But for myself, I would leave it alone.'

A Jamaican housewife behind him was closing her eyes and shaking her head at me, endorsing my opinion, so I stuck to it firmly. 'I want it shortened,' I said, 'and I shall have it shortened.'

'Very well, sir. But for myself, if it was me. . . .' He departed, muttering to himself.

This modern use of the personal pronoun is ridiculous. It's as bad as 'speaking personally'. How else are people speaking if not personally?

15 May

To Radio London for a phone-in programme which turned out to be rather embarrassing. They warned me in advance, 'You may get people on the line with some awkward questions. If you think it's getting unpalatable, give us a hand signal and we'll cut them off and go to another caller.'

Everything was going quite well until a woman came on and said, 'Hello . . . Kenneth, I wanted to question you.'

'Yes madam, what is your question?'

She said, 'The other day I was coming round Russell Square with my little girl and she asked you if you would sign her autograph book, and you said you were too busy and in a terrible hurry. You wouldn't even stop to sign an autograph for a little girl. I was very annoyed.'

'Into every life,' I replied, 'a little rain must fall and you were obviously drenched.'

I quickly signalled for the next caller who immediately said, 'That didn't sound like you. You were quite rude to that poor lady.'

'There are occasions in our lives,' I answered, 'when we don't behave as we should. It's what makes us human. No one goes around continually behaving like a paragon. There's a time and a place for autographs and Russell Square isn't it. She should come to my book-signing sessions. I'd welcome her there.'

'Oh – you've changed your mind?'

'The man who cannot change his mind is in danger of losing it altogether.'

I thought I extricated myself from a tricky situation with style, but afterwards the producer said, 'You shouldn't attempt to argue. When it comes to programmes involving the public you've got to be very careful. You must accept their strictures with grace.'

'Oh Grace! Yes, next time I'll bring her with me', I retorted, 'as long as she doesn't interrupt my intellectual Flo!'

16 May

Saw Les Dawson on television tonight. I remember meeting him backstage at the National when we were both doing a charity show. He walked onto the stage of the Olivier Theatre, looked around the auditorium and said, 'Yes, it's very prepossessing isn't it? Reminds me of a sort of high-class Wimpy bar.' It's a wonderful summing-up of that dire building. Les always amuses me and I particularly liked his remark at a theatre-awards ceremony when he told the audience, 'The recession never affected me. I was a flop when we were prosperous.'

Felt like a requiem tonight, but couldn't decide which one, the Mozart, the Verdi (which I think is a bit theatrical), the Fauré or the Brahms. Settled for the last. Am utterly in sympathy with Brahms's particular brand of north German melancholy. I suppose it must be the Celt in me.

18 May

To Shepherd's Bush and walked to the studios where I was to record the *Just William* stories for Argo. The producer said, 'I have set aside a day for this.'

I said, 'I think you're being very optimistic – all these stories in one day?' In the event, he turned out to be right. We did two in the morning, but by twelve-thirty my stomach was rumbling and the sound engineer said, 'It sounds like faulty plumbing. We'd better break.'

I was taken to lunch in a trattoira. I could have done without 'O Sole Mio' sung while serving the spaghetti sorpresa, but I was too hungry to complain. Went back in the afternoon to complete the recording. The producer picked me up several times on pronunciation and grammar and again he was right. It took me back to another time I did a recording for the BBC when the producer said, 'You're saying s*a*ltatory. Isn't it salt*a*tory?'

'I said, 'No, it's s*a*ltatory. I always say s*a*ltatory.'

'I think you'll find. . . .'

'No, no, no – it's s*a*ltatory,' and I was so firm, it was accepted. When I got home, out of sheer curiosity, I looked it up and found that it *is* saltatory.

We live and learn – and die and forget it all.

21 May

Got a postcard today from Stanley in St Lucia. It shows a brown and gnarled old fisherman at work sewing his nets by the seashore. On the back he's scrawled, 'I think I've overdone the make-up, but the *petit point* is coming on a treat.'

Like his *bon mots*, his postcards always make me laugh. They never go too far, unlike those of Robert Helpmann, who once sent me a picture of the fertility god, Bez, holding this enormous phallus, with the comment on the back, 'These foolish things remind me. . . .' That postcard was delivered together with a parcel of books, so I had to open the door to meet the postman. He shoved the lot into my hand, saying slyly, 'I hope you can bear the weight.' I smiled uncomprehendingly and only when I looked at the postcard did I understand the double-entendre.

27 May

On a radio show the other night I said, apropos of gooseberry fruit cup, that each berry must be goosed individually. Today I got a rude postcard:

> You obviously know nothing about the preparation of gooseberry fruit cup. The berries are not goosed; they are trodden. Goosing only leads to frightened fruit and shrunken palates. Your statement can only harm the export of British domestic wines, which can hold their own anywhere in the world, providing they don't travel. Yours sincerely, Freda Fuggle.

Obviously this is Maudie Fittleworth getting her own back. Not to be outdone, I replied immediately and at length:

> I know that already. All wine is made by treading grapes, apart from champagne, which is the same thing as ordinary table wine, except these monks blow a lot of bubbles through it. Then, of course, you've got different wines for different foods. Red for meat, white for fish, and rosé for foods you're not sure about, such as chicken-and-ham pie, bacon-and-egg or your fishcake that looks like a rissole. Choosing the right wine for the right food often frightens a lot of people in restaurants. 'What goes with Aylesbury duck?' you hear the lady at the table ask the man.
>
> 'Well your Aylesbury drake, of course,' comes the reply.
>
> 'Of course,' she giggles. 'Oh Fred, you are a card,' and they both laugh to cover their mutual embarrassment.

They go right through the wine-list and end up with a couple of milk stouts because they can't pronounce Châteauneuf-du-Pape.

Sometimes you sit next to one of those gullible secretaries being entertained by her boss, who says? 'Well, Muriel, I'm on the fish and you're on the game, so I think it leans towards a claret – the Château Beauregarde, I fancy.'

She always says, 'Yes, so do I.' Stupid nit, she'd agree with anything. She thinks a sauce boat is an insult on the Woolwich ferry. She's got no idea what to do and when the waiter comes back and shoves a bottle under her boss's nose, she thinks there's going to be a punch-up. She doesn't know that the man's supposed to approve the label. He looks profound and says, 'Ah yes, the Beauregarde '79. I think this will amuse you, Muriel. It's got a light bouquet, with an incredible backlash.'

She thinks, 'Hello, the girls in the office never mentioned that,' and tries to rise above it with a quip, 'Yes, it's nice, the odd backlash.'

Then he starts tasting it. That's a technique in itself. He takes a mouthful and swills it round his palate as if he's trying to find a loose filling and then remarks, 'Ah, feminine to begin, masculine to end.'

She sayd, 'Oh you make it sound so intriguing. Can I have a drop?'

'I should finish your milk stout first,' he advises.

'Oh yes,' she says, hiccuping, 'I forgot.'

By this time he's in full flow. 'Wine can turn the simplest meal into a banquet. I remember when I was with Monty coming up through Calabria, this peasant creature took us in and gave us a bit of old black pudding – filthy muck, but washed down with a rough Chianti, it tasted like ambrosia. Ah, Muriel, when will we see such halcyon days again?'

All Muriel can say is, 'Glub, glub,' because by now she's fallen face forward into the minestrone. He doesn't realise she's not going to stay with him. In fact, she can hardly stay at the table. So he pours her into a taxi with the rest of the Chateau Beauregarde and she floats off to Finchley, while he ends up with a wife in Wanstead who says, 'You're early, aren't you?'

'Well., er . . . the board-meeting broke up earlier than I expected.'

'Yes,' she says, 'the dinner's a bit burned, but there's a lovely bottle of Chateau Beauregarde. It's got a very interesting backlash,' and she lets him have it right in the moosh.

I signed the letter 'Wine-lover, Wincanton', but doubt whether she'll see through the disguise.

30 May

To Osteria Lariana for dinner tonight with Stanley. Several actors were there. My greeting them with extravagant cries of 'Darling' brought a rebuke from a man seated at a nearby table. He said, 'It's easy to tell you're all actors. You're so insincere. You use expressions like "darling" and "love" with abandon, but hardly any of you mean what you say. You're always in costume.'

'So are the police,' I replied 'But if they were naked, no one would obey them.'

June

1 June

I received a letter today from a man in Manchester thanking me for *Acid Drops* and including an F. E. Smith story I hadn't heard before.

The famous advocate had called two witnesses for the defence: one was a joiner, the other a publican. The joiner was totally incompetent and the prosecuting counsel made mincemeat of him. The publican, on the other hand, spoke succinctly and was an admirable witness.

At the end of the proceedings, the judge said to F. E. Smith, 'Your joiner hardly aided your case. He was the most incompetent witness I've come upon in any court. I am amazed that you should have produced him at all. Whereas the publican I found enlightening. Certainly the court was able to glean the necessary information from him. Why did you produce two such contrasting witnesses?'

After a silence, F. E. Smith rose and said, 'Well, m'lud, it was to illustrate the difference between the bench and the bar.'

I thought that was charming.

2 June

Went to the chiropodist today. 'This convoluted nail really requires an operation', he said. 'You'll be given a local anaesthetic. You're conscious throughout, but they cut the nail in such a way that it no longer exerts any pressure on the skin. It always works. It'll be a great improvement, but you'll have to see a specialist.'

And I said, 'Yes, it's always a specialist today, isn't it? The world moves further and further towards specialization. Eventually everyone will become better and better at less and less.'

To which he replied, 'Yes, until somebody becomes superb at bugger all.'

'Quite so,' I said, 'but in the meantime I'll carry on with my convolution.'

'It sound like a title for one of your films,' he laughed.

'Yes,' I retorted. 'And they need careful cutting too.'

4 June

When I went to the dentist today, I rose from the chair, pressing my hands down on the arms to elevate myself, and winced with pain. He said, 'What's the matter?'

'I've got this lump in my hand,' I told him, 'and every time I put pressure on it, it hurts.'

He said, 'Show it to me.' I put the palm out, he looked at the lump and said, 'You should see someone about this.' So I shot round to Dr Clarke, who said, 'Yes, it should be looked at. You've not told me about this before. I'll send you to a specialist.'

Lackaday and rue, there's no avoiding them!

8 June

Went to the hospital yesterday where a group of white-coated young men, standing round the surgeon, examined my lump.

'Have you any ideas?' he asked them.

One cried, 'Yes, sir, ganglion.'

'That's interesting,' said the surgeon. 'Interesting – ganglion. Mm. Anyone else got any ideas?'

Another student called, 'Neuroma?'

'Yes . . . have you anything further to add to that?'

'Well, I .. I think it's a fibroid neuroma.'

The surgeon seized upon that and said, 'That's it. Fibroid

neuroma. You are quite right.' Then, turning to me, he said, 'You have got a fibroid neuroma,' as though I'd come into money.

'Oh good,' I said, 'what happens now?'

'It must be removed, because it's a nerve centre, you see,' he explained. 'That's why the pressure results in pain. Now where is the registrar?'

The registrar was sent for and the surgeon asked, 'When is a bed available for this man to have his neuroma removed?' The registrar named a date about six months hence. 'I can't wait that long', I expostulated. 'As Shakespeare says, "there is a tide in the affairs of men, which taken at the flood lead on to fortune" and. . . .'

'Oh, shut up,' he said. 'Come tonight.'

Once I'd been put to bed, a man came and sat beside me and said, 'Show me your lump, I am the doctor.' I showed it to him and he got out a ball-point pen and said, 'I will draw an arrow, so that when you are wheeled to the operating theatre, this will point to the place where they are to operate. Do you see?' and he drew an arrow on my palm.

I was lying there, looking at this huge arrow, when a nurse came in and announced, 'Bath-time. Everyone has to have a bath.'

'What are you talking about, bath? I've only just arrived in the hospital. I had a bath this morning.'

'No, no, everyone has to bath. It's a rule of the hospital. Come along, come along!' and I was bundled out of bed and shoved into a bath. Needless to say, the arrow vanished in the water. Then I was taken back into the ward where I was given pentathol, apparently to make me calm. I kept saying, 'My arrow's gone,' because I thought people should know, since a doctor had taken the trouble to draw one in the first place. But the pentathol had rendered me drowsy, so I was sounding more and more bizarre. When the porters got me onto the trolley to wheel me away I heard them saying,

'He's raving!' but I knew I wasn't and kept on shouting: 'I'm supposed to have my arrow! I should have an arrow. My arrow's gone.' One of them laughed: 'It's his guilty past. He thinks he's a convict.'

When I came to after the operation, my hand was suspended in a cradle and the pain was dreadful. I was also laughing a lot. I called, 'Will somebody come and help me, I'm in great pain,' and then roared uncontrollably.

A nurse came, took one look at me and said, 'You've had too much nitrous oxide. It's made you hysterical.'

'Yes,' I replied, collapsing with laughter all over again.

Pills were brought and I went off to sleep. When I woke I was asked to give the name of a dependent relative. 'You cannot be discharged,' I was told, 'unless a person who is responsible accompanies you from the premises. You understand what would happen if you left and fell over, for example? We would be responsible. So you must send for someone. Have you anyone who is a dependent?'

'Yes,' I said, 'my mother,' quite forgetting that she herself had recently fallen over while wheeling her trolley for the WVS at St Mary Abbott's Hospital. This resulted in a hairline fracture and she'd had the entire leg encased in plaster. However, she came, limp and all and when we left the hospital today my hand was in a vertical sling, and she was teetering on her broken leg. We hobbled out together, pathetic advertisements for the NHS.

13 June

Had to go to the TV Centre for a show called *Theatre Quiz*. It was all as I had feared. I didn't know the answers and looked very foolish. I'd spoken in dread to the producer and had been told, 'Don't worry, the questions will be on subjects familiar to you.' In the event I knew none of them.

It reminded me of going to the Playhouse for the Comedy Team against the Brain of Britain Team. The quiz was chaired by Robert Robinson. At the beginning I turned to the audience and said, 'I wish I knew the answers in advance, because I don't want to look like a fool.'

Robert Robinson called out, 'Too late, Kenneth, nature's already seen to that.' He got the biggest laugh of all and I was left with *omelette sur le visage*.

14 June

Michael Anderson telephoned to wish me *bon voyage* for the Australian trip (I'm promoting *Acid Drops* and appearing on the Parkinson show in Sydney). He said, 'You do get about: yesterday Shepherd's Bush, tomorrow the Antipodes.'

'I'm worried,' I said. 'I'm like a rare wine. I shouldn't travel.'

'Nonsense,' he replied, 'you'll go very well out there. They've seen all your films and heard your broadcasts. It'll be home from home. You'll have them eating out of your hand.'

'I hope not,' I said. 'It's only just out of the sling.'

15 June

Up at 7.30. To Terminal Three, where I sat desolate and alone in the first-class lounge, feeling stared at and alien.

Boarded the plane at 9.00 for Australia. Refused breakfast because I knew that otherwise it was going to be an endless round of eating all across the world.

16 June

I was right. So far I've had Boeuf Wellington in Muscat, belly of pork in Brunei and Chicken Kiev in Singapore. No fresh fruit, so I fear the constipation will be horrendous. Talk about eastward bound – I'll be bound for life.

17 June

The plane arrived in Sydney at six o'clock in the morning. I got a taxi to the Town House Hotel. 'Alas, I have no money,' I told the driver, and he applied the brakes with alarming speed.

'What do you mean, you got no money?'

'I'm only carrying travellers' cheques.'

'Well, I don't want travellers' cheques. I'll drive you back to the airport where there's a bureau and you can cash them. I'm not driving someone who can't pay.'

'Don't be ridiculous. When we get to the hotel, they will give me money.'

He seemed to doubt this but when we arrived, I asked the receptionist to pay. The man was given his seven dollars and he looked at me with renewed respect.

I went up to my room to find flowers and iced champagne, neither of which I fancied before breakfast. Telephoned by David Lyle, the researcher from the Parkinson show who came over later for toast and coffee. 'We'll have to go over the material you'll be using,' he said 'because we mustn't repeat anything. Don't forget that a lot of the London Parkinson shows have been seen over here. So we don't want to use any of the stories you've already told.'

I suggested I might talk about the débacle in *Hotel Paradiso* where I came on stage with my flies undone and Alec Guinness pushed me behind a potted palm for the entire scene, but David interrupted: 'No, Harry Belafonte used a gag about the flies. You'll have to scrub that.' I outlined some of the other anecdotes I could use, but I must admit, sitting there with this stranger, it all sounded very unfunny and he said ominously, 'Audiences, you know, sense when there's no confidence in the delivery. They can feel the inhibition and then the whole thing clogs up.'

'Oh yes,' I agreed. 'That reminds me –' and I swallowed another laxative pill.

18 June

David Lyle came at 10.45. We met Michael Parkinson and talked about the format of the show. He warned me that, unlike London, we have to allow for six commercial breaks.

'Won't that be an awful hold-up?' I asked.

'No,' said David. 'Since you've been on those laxatives you'll need all the breaks you can get!'

I laughed incontinently.

In the evening we had dinner at the Yellow Room. Michael's very likeable and very patient. I'm afraid I went on and on, but he bore it all sympathetically. I know why I'm on edge, I feel I've got to prove myself out here. Until I actually face an Australian audience and know how I'm going to go, at the back of my mind lurks this horrible suspicion that out here my style may not work in the same way as it does in London.

19 June

A sleepless night. Feeling terrible, eye trouble, gum trouble, tight piercing pain across the chest. Don't think I've ever arrived in such a bedraggled and spiritless state to do a job anywhere.

Walked around the area in the morning and was accosted by prostitutes. It was only ten o'clock. 'Would you like a joint?' I was asked.

'No, no, thank you.' I replied. I only realized later she meant drugs, not meat. And a drunken old loon peed into a rubbish bin in the middle of a busy street.

When I returned, I said to the hotel receptionist, 'I was accosted by a tart and I saw an old man urinating in the street. It was only 10.00 in the morning.'

'Oh well, you're in King's Cross,' he said. 'That's the Bohemian area – like your Soho in London.'

'On the contrary,' I said, 'I've walked through Soho at all hours, and at 10.00 in the morning you're neither accosted nor do you see people relieving themselves. Soho's not like that. You do have a bizarre picture of the metropolis.'

Then I went off to meet Michael for lunch. I told him about the things that I'd seen in the area and he said, 'Of course, it's very way-out, it's the red light district of Sydney.'

I said, 'I thought they could do with some blue ones. The police should be much more in evidence.'

20 June

Got taken to a most extraordinary night-club – an old building in one of the sleazier parts of King's Cross. Everything was very dark. I could just see the outline of a bar, where we got drinks, but I gradually became aware of a giant screen showing what was obviously a pornographic film. I said to my host, 'I really don't think I should stay here, because I am a very well-known face and this isn't the sort of ambience in which I should be found.'

'Don't worry,' he said, 'Don't worry about a thing. It's so dark up here, no one would ever know you. You won't be recognized.'

I was standing there, nervously clutching my glass of Australian wine and looking at the screen, which was indeed diverting, when I was suddenly approached by an enormous Australian, who said, 'Hello, Kenny, I know your mother! How is she? And how's Sybil? And her old chum Mabel? And Nelly Trigger?' all of whom are indeed friends of my mother. I couldn't believe my ears.

'Oh yes,' he continued, 'I met Louisa in Tenerife. As a matter of fact, we shared the plane going over. We had a marvellous time. She told us some hilarious stories, especially the one about the number 30 bus.'

My mother had obviously told him the sixteen-inch saga. It seemd incongruous to be discussing the Balls Pond Road in the centre of Sydney. I know Michael Anderson said it would be home from home here, but this is ridiculous.

21 June

To the studio for the Parkinson Show with Marti Caine and the novelist Colleen McCulloch. Did a run-through, got made up and there was an awful wait while I watched the others doing their stuff. I went on eventually, talked about my army experiences in Singapore and told one of my favourite stories about Orson Welles in *Moby Dick*. Gordon Jackson played the lead in it and his opening line was, 'Call me Ishmael. Long ago I had a dream. . . .' Orson Welles was bawling instructions through a megaphone from the stalls and, at the dress-rehearsal, on the line 'Call me Ishmael,' he shouted, 'And if a man answers, hang up.'

Later, when Gordon came on as the first-mate, with

Patrick McGoohan as Starbuck and Wensley Pithey as third mate, to begin their scene, Orson called out 'You look like the Andrews sisters,' at which we all fell about with laughter.

When the dress-rehearsal came to a close, we were all given drinks by Orson and while we feasted on hampers of food he'd got from Fortnum and Mason's, a man appeared from heaven knows where and began fawning over Orson, saying, 'You are one of the greatest, and I've seen them all, John Gingold, Billy Dainty, I've met 'em all, wonderful people. But you are the greatest.'

'Thanks. . . .,' Orson muttered.

'No, I mean it,' the man continued, 'and I have personal knowledge, because I was a director of Abbot's Plays.'

'Sounds like a monastery,' Orson said in an aside to me.

'What d'you say? I heard that. What d'you say? You made a crack, didn't you? I can hear, you know.' Whereupon the man did a complete *volte-face* and said, 'I'll tell you what I really think of you, you fat-gutted old fool,' and he began a terrible tirade, from which Orson was barely able to escape without coming to blows.

This led to my telling Michael about Orson doing an open-stage production of *Julius Ceasar* in tandem with *Antony and Cleopatra*. During a matinée of *Julius Ceasar*, in the middle of the stabbing scene, the stage-door opened and in walked an actress named Madie Christians. She was in full view of the audience, as there was no scenery. She wasn't in that production at all and, forgetting there was a matinée, had come back to retrieve something she had left on stage from the morning's rehearsal of *Antony and Celopatra*. She was dressed in a leopard skin coat and was carrying a string shopping-bag full of groceries. Far from evoking ancient Rome, Madie epitomised Fifth Avenue. Realizing she had walked into a performace of *Julius Ceasar*, she went down on one knee and placed her hand upon her forehead, looking suitably doom-stricken, like some latter-day Cassandra.

The changes between scenes were effected by the lights alone and when these dimmed for the end of the stabbing scene, Madie Christians tried to make her way back to the stage-door, got hopelessly entangled with the senators manoeuvring into their next position, so that when the lights returned she was still there with her shopping bag and her leopard-skin coat! Orson said she never got off. During that entire performance the audience kept spotting her kneeling in different parts of the stage.

22 June

Various phone calls congratulating me on the show last night. My fears about an alien audience were unjustified. Flushed with success, I descended to the hotel bar for a celebratory drink, where I bumped into my old chum, Bill Kerr. He greeted me affectionately, then ruined it all by saying: 'We're the last of Hancock's Half-Hour, Kenny. Tony's gone, Sid's gone, Hattie's gone, there's only the two of us left.' I felt as though I were teetering on the brink of the grave myself.

We talked about the time we walked through Kensington Gore with Tony on the way to his flat, and how a bus had stopped and the driver had called out, 'Hello Tone', before getting down to shake Tony by the hand. The cars behind started hooting at the parked vehicle. Drivers alighted to protest, then, recognizing Tony, they all besieged him with handshakes and requests for autographs. Bill said, 'That must have been one of the biggest traffic jams that never had anything to do with a road accident.'

Bill said he'd been filming *Gallipoli*. 'You've got to wait till you're old before they start giving you good parts.'

He told me a story about a speaker at an exclusively male dinner. His wife asked him what he was speaking about and he lied, 'It's a talk about flying.'

'But you know nothing about flying,' she said.

'Oh, that's all right,' he told her. 'I can mug it up. You can get everything from books.'

In fact he treated the gathering to a series of outrageous sexual anecdotes, which delighted everyone enormously. Later on a member of the audience met his wife and congratulated her, 'Your husband spoke brilliantly. Everyone was delighted.'

'I don't understand it,' she said. 'He's only been up twice. The first time he was sick and the second time it blew his hat off.'

23 June

Had to go to a huge store, called David Jones, for a book signing. I was full of trepidation for, while I'd had very well-attended signing sessions in England, I wasn't at all sure about how I was going to be received out here.

The manager met me and took me through the shop, up various escalators to the book department where I was delighted to find a queue of customers awaiting me. I was very impressed by the store. 'This is sumptuous,' I said to the manager. 'It reminds me of Selfridges.'

'We *prefer* to be compared with Harrods,' he said.

The session was a great success. This came as a considerable relief to me, having heard from another comic how he had once sat with his pile of books waiting for a prospective buyer and the only person who turned up was a bedraggled old tramp who tottered onto the rostrum, felt the thickness of one of the books and demanded, 'how much are you asking for this?'

'Er, £5.95.'

'Yes, you are a bloody comedian,' snorted the tramp and he stomped away.

24 June

Taken to a very swish restaurant called Butler's. An English lady came to the table and said, 'I saw you on the Parkinson Show. It was very good, delightful for us, because, you see, I'm English. We understand the nuances. I don't think the locals here got a lot out of it.'

'Thanks a hump,' said David Lyle, my Australian host, who afterwards confided, 'They still think of us as colonials.'

David's brother, Richard Lyle, took me to the Balmain area, where some of his friends have a house. There was a log fire, dogs and cats snoozing. It was all very pleasant. A couple called Michel and Michelle (very disconcerting) were there. He spoke perfect French and Walloon. I said to him, 'You're one of the most fluent polyglots I've ever met. What do you do?' – thinking he would be some sort of academic.

'I wash wool,' he said.

I was staggered, and told him: 'You could have pulled quite a lot of it over my eyes.'

25 June

Trip to Bondai beach which was exactly like Cornwall. We might have been in Newquay. Beautiful warm weather with the sun sparkling on the blue sea and the endless expanse of golden sand winding round a lovely bay.

'What a pity it is you're here in winter,' said my host.

'You call this winter?' I echoed. 'You don't know how well off you are.'

Back to the hotel and a TV crew arrived in my room to shoot a sequence for a show called *Rat Bags*. They said, 'Tell us a funny story, just any funny story straight into camera, because this show is a collection of items and each week we like to have a personality telling one of his favourite stories.'

So I looked into the camera and said, 'Well, this story concerns a rather unlovely creature, who confessed that she never succeeded in attracting anyone. "Even when I go into my local," she said, "I sit, having my drink alone and no one comes near me." A friend told her to do something eccentric so that she would be the cynosure of all eyes. The following night she entered the pub with a parrot on her shoulder. Sure enough, a crowd gathered round, full of excitement and curiosity. To the man standing nearest, she said, "If you can guess what that is on my shoulder, you can kiss me."

He faltered and said, "Er . . . a crocodile?"

' "That's near enough, buster," she said, and grabbed him.'

26 June

Interview in the hotel with a newspaper man, at the end of which he said, 'How much longer do you give yourself?' (He meant in the business, but instinctively I felt horribly old.)

Among other things, he said, 'Last week we ran an article on comedy written by one of our Australian comedians. In this he described you as a Pommy poofter. What's your reaction to that?'

'I view the remark with Olympian indifference,' I said, and disappeared in a flurry of talcum powder.

27 June

To the studio for another *Parkinson Show* where he asked me about working with Tony Hancock. I said that much had been written about his morbidity and as Australia was the country in which he had taken his life I didn't want to dwell on that side of his career. I chose instead to tell them about a delightful occasion at a packed Camden Theatre, when we were recording the radio show *Hancock's Half-Hour*. Halfway through the producer announced, 'We've lost the line to Broadcasting House. Will you fill in with some other material and we'll return to the script when we get the line back.'

Tony said to Sid James, Hattie Jacques, Bill Kerr and myself, 'You go off into the wings and each take a turn, running on doing interruptions.'

The first one was Bill Kerr, who ran on and said, 'I went to Smithfields and got a pound of meat for only fivepence.'

Tony: 'You got a pound of meat for only fivepence? What was it, mutton?'

Bill: 'No, rotten.'

Then I came on sprinkling 'woofle dust' saying, 'I am sprinkling woofle dust to kill the wild elephants.' Tony was supposed to say, 'But there are no wild elephants round here,' to which I was to say, 'No and this isn't real woofle dust.'

I came on and pranced about the stage, miming throwing the woofle dust about, and he said nothing. The audience started giggling and eventually I went close to him and said, 'Ask me what I am.'

'We all know what you are,' said Tony and got the biggest laugh of the evening.

In the hospitality room after the show one of the other guests, a painter and something of an authority on the bush country, Jack Absolom, confided to me, 'What Mike needs on his show is not a load of Pommies but a few real characters from the bush country. I could introduce him to dozens of wonderful characters, people who say of their kids, "I grewed him." That'd be wonderful. That's what people want to hear.' Privately I thought that wasn't at all what people wanted to hear, but hadn't the courage to say so to his face.

28 June

After a sleepless night wondering what people really did want to hear, I was just getting off this morning when the phone rang: 'The boat trip's on, we're all waiting.'

I longed to say no, but in the event it was all very pleasant. We were taken on board Sir James Hardy's yacht, the *Nerida*, and sailed around the harbour and the islands, sipping champagne and eating a delightful cold lunch of turkey and chicken. They gave me the tiller because I told them I had been in the Sea Cadets, and since I didn't want to put down my drink or my cigarette, I steered with it between my legs. They took a photograph of me, which came out rather embarrassingly.

We told each other stories during the trip. 'The conditions here,' I said to them, 'are a lot different to my first sea voyage which was aboard the SS *Devonshire*, a dreadful troopship. Practically the only consolation was the odd occasion when I had the luxury of the first-class lounge in which to hold auditions for the shows I produced. In one of these I cast a handsome lieutenant, who sang 'Monterey' with affecting charm. The pianist confided to me afterwards, 'Fancies himself, but he can sing. And he'll go down well with the nurses.' By the time the show was being performed he'd proved to be right on both counts: the singing was greeted with vigorous applause, and the lieutenant was the blue-eyed boy as far as the ladies were concerned. Whether performing, playing deck-games or chatting by the ship's rail, this young baritone was always surrounded by a bevy of female admirers. His success, on and off stage, enlarged his confidence and by the time we rehearsed the second edition of the show, it was he who was suggesting the running order, choosing two spots in each half, and leading the finale.

By the time we arrived in Bombay, he was the toast of the troopship. On departure day, I was by the gangplank, and saw him disembark. As usual, the ladies were clustered round him and he was saying his goodbyes. It was during this that one of the nurses became tearful, begged the use of a handkerchief and the smiling lieutenant pulled one out of his pocket. As he did so, several contraceptives cascaded round his ankles and the admiring group drew back a pace. In the ensuing silence, there was a rush of other ranks to pick up the little purple packets. Soldiers scurried forward chorussing, 'Here you are sir!' and 'Here's another one, sir!' as they pressed all the tiny envelopes back into his hand. The Lieutenant's handsome features reddened as he silently accepted the offerings, but, though somewhat fixedly, he still managed to smile.

'Told you he fancied himself,' said the pianist out of the corner of his mouth.

'Yes,' I admitted, 'and from the looks of things, several others as well.'

29 June

I was to leave at 2.30 pm, but the hotel receptionist rang to say that the plane was delayed. 'You report tonight, instead of this afternoon, at nine o'clock. You're on a BA flight to Melbourne and you'll have to wait there in the transit lounge until 2 am, but they cannot guarantee first-class all the way, only to Abu Dhabi.'

I said 'To hell with that,' and got on to Quantas and rebooked the flight with them. It set off on time and I drank brandy and soda to settle my stomach.

I sat next to a belligerent man who said, 'I'm Australian. Why should your Queen have the power to appoint Governor-Generals who can sack our Prime Minister?'

'For the same reason that Victoria had to arbitrate over the Argentine-Chilean border,' I countered.

I was about to enlarge on this when I was interrupted by a drunken bank manager who said, 'You have a wonderful talent. I'm only a common bank manager on thirty thousand a year.'

I replied, 'I'd be delighted to be common on thirty thousand a year.' People imagine that actors earn vast sums. If they knew the truth, they'd be greatly disillusioned.

I woke up after the brandy with an awful pain in my neck and asked the steward, 'Will you fetch an osteopath?'

He said, 'We don't carry one, I'm afraid.'

'Really, the service is appalling,' I replied. 'I should have waited for BA.'

30 June

Arrived at Heathrow. Got a taxi home. Coped with an enormous backlog of mail. The Australian shampoo which I purchased out there is superb. I must find out if I can get it in England.

Radio London rang almost at once. 'Will you host a show for a week in August?'

I said, 'All right, as long as it doesn't conflict with *Just A Minute* dates.' They said they would check.

Wrote letters of thanks to all the people who were kind to me in Sydney. Went to Alonso's for dinner and fell asleep in the car on the way home. Jet-lagged, obviously.

July

2 July

Went to my osteopath at Marble Arch, Johnnie Johnson. As usual he fixed my neck with incredible efficiency. It was all over in about twenty minutes.

I got the bus back and a woman sitting by the door shouted, 'They're all fools in Hyde Park! Bird droppings all over them and serve them right.' She seemed to be addressing all and sundry and her eyes were wide with provocation. 'I live round here,' she continued, 'but I never set foot in that place. I don't want bird droppings over me and I don't want to see the other kinds of birds either. I know what they're dropping, don't worry yourself! It's disgusting. You can see it going on at all hours: there ought to be a law.'

After the initial surprise, the other passengers were smiling sympathetically at each other and the conductor came down the stairs calling 'Fares please!'

She cried out again, 'I wouldn't go to Hyde Park if you paid me.'

He didn't look surprised. 'We've just past it,' he said.

'Good job, too,' she retorted. 'I don't want bird droppings all over me. Stains on your clothes; you can't get them off.'

'You'll get off if you don't pay your fare.'

'That's all right, I live near here.'

'I don't care where you live. You have to pay your fare.'

'I've got no money on me!' Then her mouth widened in a sudden smile as she added, 'You can search me.'

The invitation obviously held no attraction for the conductor and he said with weary finality, 'You'll have to get off.'

She jumped up with amazing agility and stood on the platform. 'Suits me. This is my stop anyway,' and as the bus stopped she waved coquettishly, alighted, and began haranguing the queue with dire warnings about the dangers of Hyde Park and bird droppings.

The conductor raised his eyes to heaven. 'Ain't it marvellous?' he said and went on with his collection.

This is only one of many curious episodes I've witnessed on London Transport. There seems to be something about buses which encourages a volatile garrulity in certain people. On a number 12 leaving Notting Hill, I heard a swarthy young man saying to his companion, 'Your winters are so cold. I think it is very miserable. Your pound every day is going down but your prices are going up. Is very bad. I think I go back to Venezuela; is nice there, and much warmer.'

Whereupon an elderly, moustached veteran sitting across the aisle, leaned over and bellowed, 'Yes! Go back to Venezuela, why don't you? We don't want to hear your minnying and moaning! It's people like you that have brought this country to its knees. Go back where you belong. Good riddance to you!'

He was all but prodding the South American with his umbrella when a bright West Indian conductress came between them. 'Now then, guv! Settle down, settle down. We can all make it together. I don't want no rows on my bus. All right?' and the great white teeth beamed an infectious smile as she restored tranquillity. She turned and winked at all the other passengers. I think the staff of London Transport could run the United Nations; their resilience is phenomenal.

Maggie Smith once told me of an earnest young girl offering money at Baker Street station, asking for 'Bosco di San Giovanni' and getting a ticket immediately from the young Jamaican behind the grille. When Maggie asked him what the girl had wanted, he said, 'St Johns Wood. You got to interpret as well in this job.'

George Rose used to recount a conversation he overheard in a bus queue outside Broadcasting House, when a fur-coated lady confided to a friend, 'My dear, their house-warming was absolute chaos and people spilled over into some of the bedrooms. I was standing in the hallway, having a drink with Muriel and she saw it first. It was simply lying there on the stairs, in full view of everyone! Muriel was completely nonplussed and, at first, so was I, but eventually I found some cotton wool and then she got this paper napkin and we wrapped it up in that. We put it back straight away. For all I know it's lying on those stairs to this day.' George said the bus arrived at that point and it was maddening that he never learned the nature of the object. Like the Thurber cartoon, everything was left to the imagination.

I saw a lady on the 53 one Christmas who was trying to interpret the hanging decorations in Regent Street; she'd got on the bus with her husband and they were laden with parcels. She gazed out of the window of the top deck, intrigued by the coloured panels suspended across the road; they depicted the three wise kings of Orient. She turned to her husband and asked, 'What are them signs, Bert?'

He was obviously tired and uninterested, 'How the hell should I know?'

'Well, they must mean something, mustn't they?' she persisted brightly.

'They're just decorations,' he muttered, lighting his cigarette and coughing.

She fanned the air with her hand and then stopped as though inspired. 'Oh. Of course. I know what they are. Yes! They're the Sheiks of Araby!' and she seemed delighted with her own explanation.

It was also on the 53 that I heard my favourite exchange. The bus was coming to a halt and the conductor announced, 'Piccadilly, Regent Street, Shaftesbury Avenue.'

A bellicose man in a check cap descending the steps demanded, 'Did you say "Let's be having you?" '

The conductor said shortly, 'No,' and then added aggressively, 'but d'you want to make something of it?'

'Not without me strawberries!' cried the other chap and promptly jumped off the bus.

That 'readiness of conception and affluence of language' which, Samuel Johnson wrote, 'was always necessary for colloquial entertainment', is delightfully abundant on London Transport; semi-subsidised, special, and endlessly surprising. I don't know where we'd be without it.

4 July

Went down to Brighton with Paul Richardson, because it was such a pleasant day. We walked along the front and then went to the Royal Crescent and had a drink in the bar, where we bumped into Simon Gray and Harold Pinter down for their play at the Theatre Royal.

I said to Simon, 'I remember coming to your production of *Wise Child* at Wyndhams Theatre. I think it must have been about the third night, when a man in the stalls rose and shouted at Alec Guinness, who was appearing in drag, "You should be ashamed of yourself, Sir Alec. Do you hear? A knight of the realm dressed as a woman – disgraceful!" Stewards came and ushered him away while Alec continued unperturbed.

When I went backstage afterwards, Gordon Jackson told me there'd been quite a nasty moment for him, too, in the wings. Just before Gordon was due on stage, Alec dressed in his fur coat and holding a handbag, turned to him suddenly and said, "I can't go on."

"What, what's the matter?" asked Gordon.

"I've got the curse," said Alec, and Gordon giggled uncontrollably just as his cue came.'

We all laughed about that and then I followed it up with the delightful story about Gordon going down to Alec's country home, and being taken to the paddock, where Alec said, 'You must see this lovely Shetland pony we've recently acquired.' He called out 'Gordon . . . Gordon,' at which a little pony came trotting up.

'How sweet of you,' said Gordon. 'You've named him after me.'

'That's right,' said Alec, 'because everyone in the family said that he's got a nice, open, honest face, just like Gordon's.'

Gordon was very touched about it and by chance he found himself telling the tale some days later to Simone Signoret. 'Oh, that's rubbish', she said. 'When I was there, he called out "Simone . . . Simone" and the pony came trotting up. He's not responding to the name. He's coming for the carrots Alec's got in his hand.'

The Royal Crescent is a pleasant enough establishment. I was once staying there with Edith Evans when we were playing in *Gentle Jack*. We used to go back after the show and have a cold collation, because the dining-room had closed by the time the show ended. They always left one lighted chandelier over a table in the corner where a couple of tin lids were put over a curling lettuce leaf and a slice of ham. We were sitting there one night when an elderly man, who was doubling as waiter and night porter, came shuffling in. 'Hello Dame Edif,' he said, 'your partner in crime has had her grub and gone to bed.' (The lady to whom he was referring was an adviser on spiritual matters to Edith Evans, who was a Christian Scientist.) Edith took this announcement with aplomb and said, 'No . . . we can't expect everyone to keep theatrical hours.'

'That's right,' he said. 'Do you fancy a drop of wine?'

'Yes, half a bottle of Beaujolais would not come amiss.'

He winked. 'I thought you'd fancy a drop of the old Beaujolais, I'll go and see if there's some left over.' And as he departed, he broke wind violently.

Edith shook her head. 'This place has gone off terribly,' she said. 'That would never have occurred in the days of Mrs Taunt.' Then she asked me, 'Did they give you any notes after the show?'

'Yes, the producer came round and gave me a rewrite for Act III. Did you get anything?'

'Binkie [Beaumont] came into my room and told me Hardy Amies has designed some very regal constumes for me. Binkie said I should look equally regal in them. Do you think that's justified?'

'I think any cricitism of your deportment is tantamount to impertinence.'

'You're a very pleasant young man,' she said, and touched my knee, adding, 'There's no reason why the right girl shouldn't come along.'

'Don't be ridiculous,' I told her. 'I'm forty-six.'

'No,' she said, 'It's never too late.'

'It is tonight, Dame Edif,' said the porter, returning empty-handed. 'The cellar's locked. Your Beaujolais's off but I've got a couple of light ales in the larder.'

'Hardly an appropriate substitute,' muttered Dame Edith mournfully, prodding her slice of ham.

8 July

Dinner at Alan Bennett's. He gave me directions on the telephone: 'You'll know the house. There's a caravan outside.' I assumed he meant it would be parked in the street. But when I got there, the only house with a caravan outside had it in front of the door, blocking the drive. As I inched my way round it, I could see through the window a lady undressing. I looked away discreetly and rang the doorbell, desperately hoping it would open quickly. When Alan arrived I told him, 'You didn't say that the caravan was in the drive, nor that the occupant chose to undress at this hour.'

'She's a notable eccentric,' he explained, 'and the borough has twice threatened to remove the caravan and tow her away. I feel she is a free spirit and the admirable thing about her is that she will accept nothing from the state and ekes out a precarious existence in which every penny is earned. I admire thrift of that sort enormously and that independence of character.'

When I was seated with the other guests, who included Peter Cook, I said how generous it was of Alan to give this woman a site for her mobile home.

'It's nothing to do with generosity,' Peter said. 'She's a perfect burglar alarm, isn't she? Loads of these houses along here get done. They've been ransacked on more than one occasion, but the sight of her undressing, and the fumes going up from the primus and the smell of stale bacon and eggs floating over the area, is a sure way of keeping them off.'

I could well believe it.

13 July

The plumber came this afternoon and installed a new lavatory. It was only afterwards that I realized it was crooked. Obviously he didn't get the rear bend in the ceramic bowl to meet the waste-pipe at the correct angle.

When Michael came at 7.30 I showed him the lavatory. 'Look, it's crooked,' I said.

'I shouldn't worry about it,' Michael replied. 'It isn't as though you're actually going to be looking at the back of the loo all day, is it?'

'No, I suppose not,' I said, much comforted.

We went to The Tent for dinner.

14 July

The loo leaks! It's only just been installed. It's disgraceful. I rang the plumbers and they're supposed to be coming tomorrow. This kind of thing can only happen to me. Anyone else would simply get a new lavatory and it would be all right. I must be the only person in London to get flushed with failure.

15 July

Another plumber came and put in another loo. This time he placed it correctly. After fitting it, he waited for the cement to set and then tested it. He said, 'You'd better have a look and see if there's anything you're unhappy about.'

'No, it's fine,' I told him. 'It's set straight.'

'That other pan looked as though the bloke who fixed it was pissed,' he remarked.

'Well, if that were the case, he'd certainly found the right utensil,' I replied, thinking it was very amusing.

'Yeh, he couldn't fix a ball-cock,' said the plumber, dismissing thereby both his colleague and my joke.

18 July

While painting the undercoat round the new lavatory pipes, I heard a recording of Gus Elan on the radio, singing his peculiar version of 'Half a Pint of Ale' and 'It's a Great Big Shame'. My father adored all those satirical Cockney numbers and my mother was always singing sentimental popular songs. When I was very small, she used to sit me on the kitchen table to get me out of the way while she scrubbed the floor. One of her favourites was 'Are You Lonely Tonight?' part of which ran, 'Do the chairs in your parlour seem empty and bare/Do you gaze at your doorstep and picture me there?' But the way my mother elided the words, I always fancied I'd heard, '. . . chairs in your parlour, cementy and bare', and I thought the song was about a girl who loved a builder who was covered in cement and left a lot of it on her furniture.

I got a lot of the lines wrong in school hymns, too. One I always misunderstood was: 'There is a book who runs may read/Which Heavenly truth imparts'. This stumped me completely. Was May Read a shop, I wondered? Did someone run it? And what was the book? Perhaps it was a betting shop? It was all very odd. It was years later that I looked up 'runs may read' in a dictionary and found it defined as 'That which is said to be of easily intelligible exposition.'

Not when I was a child.

19 July

Went to the park with Louie. We sat in deck-chairs and listened to a rotten recital by the band – lousy music and badly played. The afternoon was very humid. People hurriedly rose from their chairs when the ticket collector appeared, and quite well-heeled cheats protested, 'I've only just sat down and anyway I was just about to leave.' It was pathetic to watch.

23 July

To Teddington Studios for *Give Us A Clue* and met Alfred Marks. We got talking about an actor who had appeared as the subject of *This Is Your Life* and I commented that hardly any of the people he worked with had turned up to sing his praises.

Alfred said, 'They baulked at such hypocrisy', and he went on to speak of the man's intolerable conceit and his awful habit of name-dropping. Apparently he had told Alfred that he'd recently sat next to Prince Philip at the Dorchester, where he'd told His Highness that his career had begun behind the green baize doors of the kitchen there. Glorying in his humble beginnings he said he used to do the washing-up in the kitchen there.

Alfred remarked to him, 'That's an odd coincidence, you know, because when I dined at the Palace yesterday, the Queen asked Philip, "Why did you spend your time talking to some dreary dishwasher at the Dorchester, you twerp?"

But Alfred said it was just like water off a duck's back. 'He didn't get any of it – he was totally lacking in self-awareness.'

I thought afterwards that would provide a lapidiary inscription for so many actors.

27 July

To Bush House for a talk show. One of the speakers was grumbling about the appalling results of modern education. I said that I had read a letter in *The Times* from a professor complaining that out of twenty undergraduates, not one of them knew that the angle in a semi-circle is a right angle.

Another guest said, 'A teacher asking a pupil, "What's the capital of Antigua?" was told, "About 50p I should think." '

For some reason, this reminded me of Les Dawson in a send-up of Dickens' *A Christmas Carol*. When the ghost of Christmas Present asked him, 'How are the Cratchits?' he replied, 'They're fine. I think that ointment's done the trick.'

31 *July*

On the way to Wembley today to visit Peter Godwin, I passed the TV studios where I'd once done the David Frost show with Ted Ray. The theme of the show was medicine and I thought at the time that Ted must have a memory like a file index, because he told joke after joke about physicians, including the wonderful one about the woman rushing into the surgery and saying to the doctor, 'Oh doctor, those hormone tablets you gave me . . . my husband's mistakenly got hold of the box and swallowed them all.'

'Don't panic,' the doctor said. 'Is he at home now?'

'Yes.'

'Well, don't worry, I'll telephone him.'

'If a woman answers, don't hang up. That'll be him.'

August

3 August

Saw Maudie Fittleworth in Boots. She was just back from her Italian holiday with Adrian. She said that on the train to Rome they met an American tourist and asked her where she was going.

'To Florence.'

'Oh, we've just passed it,' said Adrian. 'Didn't you see it? It was written up "Firenze".'

'What's with this Firenze crap? Why don't they put up "Florence"?'

It reminded me of Martin Heal's story about an American asking an Englishman sitting opposite him on an Italian train, where he was going. The Englishman told him Assisi.

'Is that a trendy resort?' asked the American.

'I'm not concerned with its tourist appeal,' replied his fellow-traveller, 'I'm going as a pilgrim to visit the birth-place of St Francis.'

'What's so special about him?'

'Well, you must have heard about him. It was an extraordi-nary life. He was a profilgate who had a dream that inspired him to renounce his wealth and possessions and care only for the poor and the sick. Indeed he became such a benign character that even birds and beasts trusted him and ate from his hand.'

'That's kind of cute, that story. That's really great. He sounds quite a guy.' When he left the train he said, 'Well, it's very nice to have met you. If you're ever in the States, you must pay a pilgrimage to my home town.'

'Where's that?' asked the Englishman.

'San Francisco,' came the reply.

Out of the mouths of babes and American tourists come anything but wisdom.

6 August

To the oculist. I felt pleased when he said, 'Your long sight is good. Six out of six. You could pilot the Concorde. But,' he added, 'you need glasses for reading.'

Afterwards I was seen by an optician, who showed me lots of frames, but all were made abroad. I said, 'Show me some English ones.'

He said, 'Most spectacle frames are either Austrian or German.'

But I stuck to my guns. 'I don't wish to patronize foreigners,' and settled for a pair made by Cambridge Opticals. I felt like that blimp in Peter Cook's sketch, who's offered *spargel im Hofrats Gemuhe*, by the waiter, who adds, 'It's flown in specially from Bonn.'

'Bloody Bosch rubbish,' explodes the man, 'as soon as they stop bombing you they start selling you their second-hand vegetables!'

10 August

Went to Radio London for a broadcast with Morecambe and Wise. Their new book is called *There's No Answer To That*. The interview flowed very well. I asked Eric whether he had to watch his diet after the heart trouble. 'Yes,' he said, 'I must steer clear of all starches, unlike someone of your build, who has no problems of that kind.'

'On the contrary, Eric,' I said. 'If you saw me naked, you'd get a shock. The belly is alarmingly protuberant and the bum is hanging in pleats.'

When I got home Louie said, 'Edith and I listened to your show. It was very good. Edith commented on your clear enunciation, she said she could hear every word.'

'Yes, that's one of the great advantages of radio,' I said.

Unlike the mishearing of the hotel porter when Dame Edith Sitwell came for her key. 'Anything in the morning, madam?' 'Only a coffin,' came the mournful reply. 'Black or white?' he asked.

13 August

Since doing that phone-in programme for Radio London, people seem to regard me as an authority on the world of entertainment. A correspondent writes today: 'Can't you do something about the appalling standards at present prevailing in T.V. I was shocked to see a programme the other night, at 10.30, in which two people were so close together you couldn't see anything between them, and they weren't even married.'

Having looked into this matter, I wrote back and pointed out to her that the two people involved *were* married, but not to each other. I hope that explains it satisfactorily for her. Anyway, she's got to expect that sort of thing if she insists on watching all-in wrestling, especially at that time of night.

15 August

Met Maudie Fittleworth again, in D. H. Evans, with Adrian in tow. She was at the sweet counter. 'I just fancy the sugar-puff balls, I've got a sweet tooth.' Privately I thought, 'It's the *only* one you've got.' Her mouth looks as though it's full of fluted plastic. Heaven knows who copes with her dentistry.

She seemed to guess my thoughts, because she admitted, 'My personal appearance is against me.'

Adrian stepped in quickly, adding, 'But she's irrepress-ible, she'll let nothing get her down.'

'She'll let nothing get her up either,' I countered, 'judging by the time she rises. When I was on tour with her, she hardly ever made the train call.'

'What irony,' cried Maudie, 'when you think what I did to pioneer female travel. I wrote *Every Girl's Guide to the Gobi*, *Damsels Up the Dolomites* and *Dollies in the Dordogne*. Oh, those were the halcyon days. I spent months soaking up the local colour.'

'Well, it's only 50p a bottle out there,' interjected Adrian.

'Are you suggesting I'm a drinker?' asked Maudie indignantly.

'Well, let's face it,' he replied, 'you're the only one who can blow on the birthday cake *and* light the candles.'

I could see there would be tears before bedtime, so I beat a hasty retreat.

17 August

Saw a lovely item in *The Telegraph* today about a boy of twelve being asked to attend a coffee morning for the Save the Children Fund. 'Why?' he enquired, 'are they becoming extinct?'

It reminded me of the beggarwoman approaching the ermine-coated lady alighting from her Rolls outside the Savoy. 'Lady, help me!' cried the crone. 'I haven't eaten for three days!' 'Well, my dear,' came the gracious reply, 'You must simply force yourself.'

19 August

Went with Michael to the Rose Garden in Regent's Park, where I sat in a deck chair and chatted to

Myrna, one of the regular sunbathers there. She said she was trying to keep up the tan from her holiday in Corfu. She showed me the photographs taken there. One depicted her holding a glass and wearing a very smart evening gown. I asked, 'Was this taken at the cocktail hour?'

She said, 'No, we were having drinks before dinner.' (I don't think she's very bright.)

Michael spoke of his hotel in Madeira. 'It was all very pleasant, but you had to get down to the terrace very early, otherwise the Germans grabbed all the dildos.'

Myrna looked mystified. I said, 'You mean the lilos.'

'Of course, what did I say?'

'Dildos.'

'Oh heavens.'

Myrna asked, 'What *are* dildos?'

'Those boats like bicycles you hire at the seaside,' I explained, craftily.

'Oh I thought they were things you buy in pornographic shops.'

'No,' said Michael, 'they're pedalos.'

20 August

Michael and I motored to Basildon, which I had not seen before; a concrete mass of windy concourses and modern tat. After that, we went on to Southend, which was bustling and invigorating. I told Michael, 'A taxi driver last week described Hendon as salubrious. I told him that the word meant "salt air" and he said, "Then the estate agents are all wrong, there's no bleeding sea round there." '

I greedily ate two plates of cockles on the front and the assistant said, 'These are Leigh cockles. We get Dutch ones sometimes and they're much bigger.'

'These are big enough for me,' I chortled.

We were joined by three big-chested girls, who asked, 'Can you get us into the theatre?'

I foolishly asked, 'How much are the tickets?' before I realized they were discussing a stage career.

22 August

Went to visit Gordon and Rona and we fell to discussing abridged names. I said, 'Ethel Merman shortened hers from Mermansky.'

'Yes,' replied Gordon, 'we talked about that with Dorothy Tutin at the Garrick the other night. I said to her, "Of course, you knocked the Khamun off yours didn't you?"'

'Dorothy Tutinkhamun!' I cried. 'Oh, it's ludicrous.'

'Not at all,' said Gordon. 'Her children say she's a marvellous mummy.'

23 August

Reading Mary McCarthy on Venice. It's a fascinating book. I remember visiting Venice and going to a glass factory there in 1963. It prompted a line I wrote for *International Cabaret* about being an apprentice glass-blower: 'I was supposed to do the bulbs on the thermometers, but one day I huffed too much and blew myself a goldfish bowl.'

24 August

Met Barry Wade, who was very funny about visiting Giovanni Patti in St Stephen's Hospital. Barry was wearing that summer outfit of his, flowered shirt and coloured trousers, which I always say looks like pyjamas. He described how he was waiting on a vacant bed, while Giovanni was being examined by the doctor behind closed curtains. 'Right, stitches out tomorrow', said the doctor, 'and you can go home. Report back in three weeks and present yourself to the out-patients' department. Very good.'

He emerged from the drapes and saw Barry on the next bed. 'You're next.'

Barry cried out, 'No, no, doctor. I'm a visitor.'

'Well, in future, dress like one,' he snapped and passed on down the ward.

25 August

At the Equity Office this morning I heard an actor complaining, 'I was up for the chorus of this panto. Last year they said I was too tall, this time they turned me down again and said I was too short. I shouted from the stage, "You don't want a dancer, you want a bit of elastic." They were furious, but I didn't care. You know it's worked out in advance.'

I understand how he feels. Auditions are ghastly. That's why actors like to send them up. Maudie Fittleworth tells an outrageous story about Finsbury Park Empire when a dere-lict tottered up onto the stage bawling an obscene piece of doggerel, until they stopped him with, 'Thank you, we'll let you know.'

But he was not to be silenced. 'Hang on a minute! I also do a baritone speciality,' and he proceeded to sing a dirty song which they also interrupted.

'No, I'm sorry, it's not what we're looking for; quite unsuitable.'

'Well, I'll do my striptease then!' he said, and started to remove his trousers.

By this time they were standing in the stalls protesting, 'Who is this dreadful old man? He must be removed! Get the stage-door keeper.'

'I am the stage-door keeper!' he yelled.

They were appalled and shouted, 'Please adjust your dress before leaving, and don't call us 'cos we'll certainly never call you.'

26 August

Had dinner with Stan Walker. We talked about our time together at the PDC (Physical Development Centre) at Bradbury Lines during the War. I asked him why he had been sent there, bearing in mind that he'd ended up in the parachute regiment. He said that he'd had trouble with fallen arches and had to have remedial exercises, and he asked me what my trouble was.

'The army had shaken their heads in disbelief over my nudity,' I told him, 'and they sent me to this gentleman in Harley Street, who looked like Bela Lugosi. He took a pint of blood off me, and then said I had anaemia.'

'Did you have anaemia?' Stan asked.

'Yes, I was graded B2 with anaemia.'

'You look all right now.'

'Of course, my blood isn't anaemic now. I've been on the Sanatogen, the iron jelloids, claret because it's heavy with iron, and I've been eating black bread. But it was different in those days. When I went back to infantry training at Carlisle I sauntered rather than charged at the sawdust-filled dummy at bayonet practice. I remember the sergeant bawled derisively, "You couldn't kill a German; you'd kiss him!"

"Yes," I shouted back spiritedly. "Love is a many-splendoured thing," and began an apologia of passive defence.

I didn't fare any better on the rifle range. My frail wrists proved incapable of directing the gun in a constant direction and after several of my bullets had scored very respectable hits on my neighbours' targets, I was ordered to leave the range and report to the canteen for tea-making. I was struggling to the field with hot tea slopping all over my denims, when an officer came along on his bicycle and said to me, "What are you doing, soldier?"

"I'm taking this tea to the rifle range, sir," I said pitifully. "The sergeant ordered me to do it."

"Put those tea urns over my handle-bars. That'll make it easier to carry. And we'll go to the range and I shall question the sergeant about this."

When we arrived, he asked the sergeant, "Did you give this soldier orders to go and get dixies of tea?"

"That's right, sir."

"Why?"

"I ordered him off the range, sir. He was a bit of a dangerous marksman."

"Look here, sergeant, the British tax-payer is forking out a lot of money to train these lads to become soldiers, not to go making tea in the cook-house. They're not paying for that. They're paying to create a powerful war machine," he said, looking at me in my bedraggled denims, "to fight Hitler and the Nazi hordes. In future, if you want tea, you'll ask the catering corps for that, and you will train Williams here to be a first-class rifleman and an expert on the LMG (light machine gun)." '

I just about learned to master a rifle, but the LMG was right out of my scope. I was forced to take both these weapons apart, clean them and get to know them inside out. As I said to Stan, I really couldn't cope until some Geordies in the barrack-room saw my draughtsmanship and asked if I would write their names on their kit-bags. My training in lithography came to the rescue, and in return for my lettering they taught me the nuts and bolts of weaponry. I've been inordinately fond of Geordies ever since.

29 August

Funny how the war still prompts so many memories. Went up to Pebble Mill today for the chat show and told my story about going on the flagship in Hong Kong in 1946. It was after the dramatized version of the Battle of Trafalgar which we broadcast on Forces Network. We were all CSE personnel, dressed in white shirts, so we appeared to be civilians. After the performance, the Admiral of the Fleet, Sir Bruce Fraser, said, 'That was simply superb and I would like you all to come back for drinks aboard the flagship.'

We were delighted and accepted with alacrity. We were taken to the docks. The sentries stamped their feet and bashed their rifle butts at the dock entrance. A lighter took us out to the cruiser *Belfast*, and we were piped aboard and taken to the wardroom. A flag lieutenant plied us with pink gins and we began chatting amiably. One of the officers asked, 'How do you like life in the colony?'

Stanley Baxter replied, 'We don't live here. We're in Combined Services Entertainment.'

'Oh, did the army engage you?' asked the officer.

'No, we're *in* the Army,' said Stanley.

'Oh . . . and what is your rank?'

'Well, I'm a sergeant,' said Stanley.

'I'm a sergeant,' I added.

And Peter Nichols said, 'I'm a sergeant, too.'

Within a minute, the drinks were out of our hands and we were being ushered unceremoniously to the ship's side. Far from being piped overboard, I distinctly heard a very loud raspberry as we passed through the dock gates a second time.

30 *August*

Reading some of the Goncourt Journal I was struck by his insistence that 'everything that happens is unique, occurring only once'. It reminded me of those Rilke lines in the Duino Elegies:

> Once and no more,
> Just once,
> Everything only for once,
> Once and no more.
> And we too, once and never again
> But this, having been once,
> Only once,
> Having been once on earth,
> Can it ever be cancelled?

I love diaries and the Goncourt is one of the best.

I remember hearing a literary programme on the radio when an author said, 'All diarists are suspect,' and talked about their diaries really being meant for publication. Mine never were. I started writing a diary in order to keep a record of what happened. But even if one writes in the hope that it will be read, does that invalidate the comment? I don't think so. I've derived enormous pleasure from the Boswell Diaries, the Goncourt Journal, the Virginia Woolf Diaries, the Macready Journal and Lucy Norton's *Saint Simon at Versailles*. The account of the Duc de Vendôme giving an audience while perched on the *chaise percée* is riotous:

> When he was in the Army, his custom was to rise rather late and at once to take his place upon the *chaise-percée*, and in this curious position he wrote his despatches and issued his orders for the

day. Anyone who had business with him, even general officers and distinguished visitors, found that was the best time to talk with him. He gradually accustomed the entire army to that indecent habit and, still sitting there, would consume an enormous breakfast with two or three boon companions, eating, talking, and issuing orders, with a large audience of bystanders. He evacuated copiously and the pot was carried away in the front of the entire company. On the days when he shaved, the same pot was used. He called this a good honest custom, worthy of the Romans, and a fine contrast to the finical ways of some other army commanders.

31 August

Went to visit Maggie at Tigbourne and she talked of seeing Peter Shaffer in America. 'You know how other people say "wild horses wouldn't drag me there"? Peter will say, "wild Circassian horses wouldn't drag me." With him no one's got a disease, they're "pestilential" creatures. The way he ornaments his stories makes them that much funnier.'

I said, 'I'll never forget Peter's story about visiting Noël Coward in Jamaica. A room had been erected on the top of Coward's house to provide a superb view of the bay. It was constructed entirely of glass, so that the panorama was immediately visible. Unfortunately the glass was not insulated. Instead of two layers, there was only one and the temperature became well-nigh unbearable. The dinner guests included Sir Hugh Foot, the Governor of Jamaica at the time, Lady Foot, John Perry and Peter. All of them were feeling the heat and perspiring visibly, but Coward seemed impervious and announced: "It's ridiculous all this non-sense about eating tropical food when you're in the tropics. The English are capable of enjoying English food wherever they are, and since you get so little opportunity to enjoy a truly English meal when you are abroad, tonight I'm giving you hot soup, followed by roast beef and my trump card is ginger pudding flambé, which I shall flambé myself, because I'm the only one who can do it properly."

When he left the room to fetch the last course, Lady Foot said, "I'm sorry, we'll have to leave. I can't take any more of this, I'm absolutely saturated."

"Yes, give our apologies to our host," said her husband, "and say we're very tired and had to leave early because of an exhausting day tomorrow."

A moment or two after they'd left, Coward reappeared, holding a blazing dish aloft and announced, "Ginger pudding flambé." Then his face dropped and he said, "Where are the Feet?"

"They couldn't take any more," said John Perry, expounding at length on their general discomfort, as the flames died around the pudding. "The temperature's unbearable in here; the poor woman was wringing wet. They had to go; they'd have passed out otherwise. They just couldn't stand the heat."

Coward eyed the burnt remains of the sweet.

"By the looks of it," he said, "neither could my ginger pudding." '

September

1 September

An outrageous postcard arrived from Maudie Fittleworth this morning. It's a picture of her surrounded by three muscle-men, with the line, 'They say I'm mad about Tom, Dick and Harry.' On the back she's written, 'I can't stand Tom and Harry.'

4 September

Some of my stuff on *Just A Minute* has upset some correspondents. There's a letter today from one irate female: 'Your vanity is insufferable, and your impertinent remarks to the chairman are uncalled for. Mr Parsons's modesty is infinitely preferable to your overweening conceit.' She is quite wrong. I am not conceited. It's just that I have a natural fondness for the good things of life and I happen to be one of them.

Dinner with Peter Stiles, who astounded me by recalling our walk through Whitehall in 1970. 'You pointed out the window in the Inigo Jones Banqueting House from which Charles I stepped out to his execution.'

I said, 'I've been reading the Petrie collection of Charles I's letters. The writing has all the beauty and simplicity of the King James Bible. The goodness of the man shines through every word.'

One of the guests commented, 'He was no match for Cromwell.'

And I pointed out that the latter was only possible because of some very rich men: 'John Hampden behind Cromwell was just as significant as Krupp behind Hitler, and both created ruthless and efficient military machines.'

'Oh, you make it sound as though Cromwell was running a junta,' he said.

'That's not a bad description of his rule,' I replied. 'Charles I raised taxes in order to run the country, and the one which triggered all the trouble was ship-money. It was perfectly legal and fair; levied on businessmen to pay for a navy which kept the sea free of pirates, so that their merchandise should have safe passage. The richest of the merchants was John Hampden and he decided to oppose the king rather than pay. He was worth over £200,000, which was a huge sum in those days, and was asked to pay £8 a year in ship money. That's what caused all the trouble; because the king chose to levy his wealthy subjects rather than borrow from bankers. McNair Wilson pointed out, "When Charles I laid his head on the block, England owed no man anything. Today the national debt amounts to £8,000,000,000," and McNair wrote that in 1937. Heaven knows what it is half a century later.'

Peter asked, 'How do you remember all this.'

'I mugged it up for *Just A Minute*', I told him. 'I read Maurice Colbourne's book *Charles the King*. Incidentally he played my father when I was Bentley Summerhayes in the television production of Shaw's *Misalliance*.'

Peter said, 'No matter how remote the connection appears with you, it always comes back to the theatre in the end, doesn't it?'

I found myself agreeing. For me it's been the source of so many riches.

7 September

Walked to Canadian Broadcasting Service where I did an interview with Mr Aldridge. He asked about humorous incidents that had occurred during the making of the *Carry On* films. The one that came immediately to mind happened during the shooting of *Carry On Doctor* and involved Hattie Jacques as the Matron and me as Dr Tinkle.

Hattie and I had arrived on the set in good time, but the others, who were supposed to be filming before us, were late. There was a delay and finally the director, Gerald Thomas, said, 'Kenneth and Hattie are here. Let's shoot their sequence first.' This was a scene involving the two of us struggling in a doorway with her saying, 'Come on doctor, let yourself go,' and me replying: 'No, I was once a weak man' to which she answered, 'Once a week's enough for anybody.'

In the middle of this struggle, the cameraman said, 'I can't shoot this, Gerry, the door-post is shaking. You can actually see it shaking in camera. You'll have to get a carpenter to put a brace on the door.'

Gerald, who was already behind schedule, thanks to the late-comers, said, 'Don't worry about it shaking. Push the door with your shin, Kenny. Keep your leg firmly planted against it and grab Hattie with your other hand. That'll keep the door from juddering.'

I had quite a job holding up both the door and Hattie and I said, 'Alas, Gerald, my legs are not what they were.'

To which Gerald replied, 'They never were much anyway,' and was about to get quite a laugh from the crew, when Hattie said, 'Don't knock 'em, Gerald. They got him here on time today, which is more than you can say for some.'

8 September

Went to the Equity Meeting where one of the councillors told me about an occasion when Sir Felix Aylmer was president of the union. There had been an altercation over a rude letter which had been received by the general secretary. Various remedies were recommended. One councillor suggested, 'This impertinent rudeness should be replied to firmly. We should reject the complaint out of hand and our letter should be written by the President, Sir Felix.'

Somebody else said, 'No, no, that can't be done, because the letter's been written to the General Secretary. You can't have a letter sent to the General Secretary, replied to by the President. It would be like writing to the Prime Minister and getting a response from the Queen.'

'I don't think I care for the casting,' said Felix Aylmer.

10 September

Met Martin Heal who told me a story about a Vietnam draft dodger. At the railway station he asked a nun to hide him under her skirts, so that he wouldn't have to board the train with the rest of the conscripts. She agreed and he secreted himself beneath the folds of her garments until the train and the roll-calling officers had departed. Then he extricated himself, thanking her profusely, adding, 'There's just one thing. I couldn't help noticing when I was under your habit, that you're built like a man.'

'That's right,' said the nun, 'I don't want to go to Vietnam either.'

13 September

Louisa has asked me to repair the family bible which has come loose at the binding. The names of his children and dates of their birthdays are written in copperplate on the flyleaf by her father, Henry Morgan, Louie told me, 'I always think of Tin Lizzie when I open that' (Tin Lizzie was the nickname all the Morgan children used for their stepmother, Eliza Cod). I asked why and she said, 'Well, after Tin Lizzie's funeral, we all went back to her house and I went to get our Dad's portrait off the wall 'cos she said I could have it and then I saw the wood lice in the back! I screamed and dropped it. Your Aunt Alice was lifting up some glasses she was going to take, Edie had some plates and the shock made them drop their stuff as well! We all ran for the door and the three of us practically got stuck in it. Oh! We did laugh afterwards. Then there was an argument about how old Tin Lizzie was and I got Dad's bible out.

I'll never forget the funeral itself. When the cortège passed her house in Sandwich Street, the drivers went slow to show respect. Then when we got to The Plumbers, the landlord came out, waving his arms to stop the hearse. He said, "We must present our tribute, she was an old customer", which was true because she fell down twice outside that pub after having too many. The first time we took her into the Royal Free, because she cut her head so badly. Anyway the landlord's tribute was the Gates of Heaven Ajar. Well, that infuriated Alice, because it was the same wreath she'd bought. She carried on alarmingly. "Only the family should give the Gates of Heaven Ajar" she kept on saying. Of course, in the end, there were two identical wreaths on the coffin. They had the shortened version of the prayer at the end, by the grave, finishing on "deliver us from evil". Well, I didn't know. No one told me. I went on saying, "For thine is the kingdom, the power and the glory . . ." and Alice was saying, "Shut up!" Then someone dropped their handbag in the hole and the grave digger had to get it out. It was a terrible mess, I can tell you.'

Went home thinking about the secret desire in all of us to laugh at solemnity. That passage in Johnson's *Lives Of The*

Poets about the funeral of Dryden strikes a similar chord:

> The procession began to move – a numerous train of coaches attended the hearse – but, good God! in what disorder can only be expressed by a sixpenny pamphlet soon after published, entitled *Dryden's Funeral*. At last the corpse arrived at the Abbey which was all unlighted. No organ played, no anthem sung; only two of the singing boys preceded the corpse. They sang an ode of Horace, with each a small candle in his hand. The butchers and other mob broke in like a deluge, so that only about eight or ten gentlemen could get admission, and those forced to cut their way with their drawn swords. The coffin, in this disorder, was let down into Chaucer's grave, with as much confusion and as little ceremony as was possible, everyone glad to save themselves from the gentleman's swords or the clubs of the mob.

And confusion over obsequies is not confined to our own country – a ludicrous example can be found in *Saint-Simon's Journal*, where he records the death of Le Grande Mlle. de Montpensier:

> A ridiculous incident occurred during the funeral service. In the middle of the proceedings, in the presence of the entire court, the urn containing the entrails, which was on a credence table, exploded with a deafening report and a sudden, intolerable stench. On the instant, all the ladies were swooning or in flight. The heralds and the psalm-singing monks blocked the doors with the rest of the escaping crowd. There was utter confusion, but most people managed to reach the garden and the

forecourts. The explosion had been caused by the fermentation of the entrails, which had been inadequately preserved. Everything was perfumed and put to right and the scare provided a laugh. Finally the entrails were taken to the Convent of the Celestines and the heart to Val de Grâce. The body was escorted to Saint Denis by the Duchesse de la Ferté, the Princesse d'Harcourt and ladies of quality.

15 September

To Thames Television to do a programme with Mavis Nicholson. She's a good interviewer; puts people at ease immediately. She must be good since she's one of the very few people ever to get Stanley Baxter talking about himself on television.

When she asked him about tidiness in the home, he admitted he liked a clinical neatness and precision. 'Mind you', he added, 'I'm not as bad as Kenneth Williams. In *his* place, you can't even move an ash-tray without raising a howl of protest.'

Talked to the camerman afterwards about the current bingo craze. There is even talk about starting it on some provincial bus services. I said, 'They'll gamble on anything nowadays, from tomorrow's rainfall, to Russian roulette.'

One of them said, 'That's been superseded by Indian roulette.'

'What on earth,' I asked, 'is Indian roulette?'

He said, 'You sit playing a snake charmer's flute, surrounded by six cobras and one of them's deaf.'

17 September

To Southampton to do a television programme. At the hotel where I stayed I was having a drink with Arthur Mullard when a stranger came up and said, 'Can I join you?'

I secretly thought of Groucho's reply, 'Why, are we coming apart?' but all I said was, 'Yes, please do,' with affected cordiality.

'I'm down here for a conference. I'm with the firm that makes Durex.'

'Oh yes?' Arthur said.

'We're doing very well, in spite of the recession.'

'That's because they're scared stiff of the pill.'

'No, people are worried about prices and inflation. Everything's going up.'

'Yes,' said Arthur, 'and so are the Durex by the sound of things.'

21 September

Had a telephone call from the people making the commercial for BP telling me, 'You'll have to have a medical.'

'A medical?' I said, 'for one day's filming?'

'Ah, well,' said the voice at the other end, 'the clients have pointed out that they'll need to insure you against premature death. They have to cover you for half a million.'

I said, 'I don't understand why. I'm not likely to drop down dead.'

'Ah, but people are dropping all the time,' he said, 'and since you'll be playing the Devil, it would be considered in the worst possible taste if they continued, after your death, to show you prancing about in Hell with horns sticking out of your head.'

'Hang on,' I said, 'No one mentioned horns.'

'Oh, didn't they?'

'No, I thought I was going to look rather suave, in evening dress with a scarlet cloak, and simply make one or two cracks about the need to conserve heat. I honestly didn't think there was anything else involved.'

'The Devil is always depicted with horns,' he said.

I said, 'Yes, he's also pictured with cloven hoofs, but they're not going to stick them on my feet, surely?'

'No, no . . . the camera won't go down that far.'

'That's just as well,' I replied, 'wearing horns is a frightening enough prospect.'

'It's quite simple,' he said, 'they're made of plastic and you won't feel a thing.'

Within an hour, I was sent to Harley Street, where the doctor said, 'It's funny, you were nine stone two when I examined you for that film *The Hound of the Baskervilles* and you're still the same weight. You don't change at all. You've kept yourself in very good condition, and, of course, that's because you don't drink and smoke.'

'On the contrary,' I said, 'I drink like a fish. You can't call me frugal when it comes to alcohol. I've been known to arrive home on the floor of the taxi.' Then I handed him the urine specimen, saying, 'As a matter of fact, there are enough bubbles in this to make it look like champagne. Cheers!'

In retrospect I realize that this is hardly the behaviour calculated to bring the theatrical profession into repute.

23 September

To the West Country for a talk about *Acid Drops* at a local literary club. They put me in a very tatty hotel. My room had one of those popping gas-fires. I went down to the basement for dinner, which consisted of water soup, followed by chicken and soggy vegetables. A mournful old lady at the next table eyed my plate enviously and loudly enquired of the waitress, 'Why can't *I* have chicken?'

She was rebuked severely. 'Get on with your stewed lamb. It's very nice.' But the elderly incumbent remained unconvinced.

I was reminded of the extraordinary occasion when Peter Cook, who was script-writing the revue, *Pieces of Eight*, and I were in the lounge of the Ship Hotel at Brighton, having coffee, when a woman began crying audibly. Everyone else in the room sank deeper into their newspapers, affecting deafness. Then a military-looking fellow, with a clipped moustache and accent to match, entered the room and told her, 'Pull yourself together, we're leaving.'

'Oh no,' she wailed, 'I just want an aspirin and a cup of tea.'

'You've had quite enough sedation as it is,' he barked. 'You've no right to enter that home. I had the devil's own job getting you out of it. What on earth made you register with them?'

'I was worn out with worry. I felt I was losing my mind. That's why I signed the form.'

'You can't go mad without permission.'

'Well, who from?'

'The rest of the family, of course; they're responsible for you, you see.'

'Well, I felt I was at the end of my tether.'

'Rubbish. People don't decay at your age. Why did you sack Hawkins? She was admirably efficient; a very capable woman.'

'I felt she was watching me all the time.'

'That was her job. And why did you sell those shares in Metal Box?'

'All those tin cans were so depressing. I saw hundreds on a rubbish dump.'

'That's where you'll end up, if you go on like this.'

At that point a uniformed chauffeur entered and she was taken protestingly to a closed car.

I said to Peter Cook, 'That was just the sort of scene that could be built into a revue sketch. But how would it end?'

He said, 'With the other people in the room lowering their papers to reveal their faces, and suddenly you see they're all mad.'

25 September

Talked today in a radio programme about the various aspects of hope that are contained in poetry and used three illustrations. One was from a Haro Hodson poem:

> Sometimes when I've been alone too long,
> I think I hear you say my name again,
> Softly as snow flakes upon a pane,
> And hope, a lunatic that should have died,
> Careers about my heart in song,
> Setting a blaze of candles there,
> To guide your way to me.

It echoes remarkably the lines about hope in *The Cenci*, where Beatrice says:

> Speak not to me of hope,
> It is the only evil that can find a place
> Upon the dark and giddy hour
> Tottering beneath us.

The other aspect I quoted was Byron:

> White as a white sail on a dusky sea,

When half the horizon's clouded and half free,
Fluttering between the dun wave and the sky,
Is hope's last gleam in man's extremity.
Her anchor parts, but still the snowy sail
Attracts our eye amid the rudest gale,
Though every wave she climb divides us more,
The heart still follows from the loneliest shore.

This is a poignant and graphic illustration of hope. I was happy to find three such disparate yet eloquent excerpts.

26 September

Dined with Jeremy Swan, who told me a curious story about a sailor receiving fivers every week from his wife, and getting no explanation for this largesse. He obtained leave and arrived home unexpectedly to find his house transformed with new carpets, new curtains, and expensive furniture everywhere. In the bedroom, his wife was lying on an expensive four-poster, while a man, dressed only in gym shorts, was exercising with bar-bells by the open window.

The sailor asked, 'Who gave you all this furniture?'
Pointing to the gymnast, his spouse replied, 'He did.'
'And who bought all the new carpets?'
'He did.'
'And who sent me all these fivers I've been getting?'
'He did.'
'Well, close the window for heaven's sake, he'll get pneumonia!'

October

1 October

To Shepperton Studios to do something I never dreamed I'd do – a visual commercial. I got into the make-up room and the girl stuck the horns on my forehead. They were far too big. I said, 'This is ridiculous. You've got them too long. I don't look like the Devil. I look like a unicorn. You'll have to cut them down.' So they got saws and hacked them until two small horns were produced, and these were stuck on with glue. Then the cloak was draped over my shoulders. It was red velvet and weighed a ton.

The horns were agony. It wasn't long before I had a terrible headache and come lunch-time the last thing I wanted to do was to go and sit in the canteen. It would have been much too embarrassing, anyway. So I sat in the dressing-room, with no food whatsoever, starving like the Devil.

The set was a vast cavern, depicting Hell, with imps lying about on the steps. The filming was relentless – shot and reshot. The set was covered in blocks of ice – the point of the commercial being that Hell was freezing over – which were very slippery. As it melted people kept falling on it. I fell over twice and ruined my shoes: the soles were practically coming away from the uppers. One of the imps nearly broke his leg when he came a cropper.

To add to my discomfort, the talons which I had to wear kept falling off and the smoke pervading the set got into my eyes and nose. I could hardly see for the tears or breathe for the noxious fumes. It was an endless bane.

Just to increase the complications, the director was floating above us on a crane camera. He and the floor manager, to whom he was supposed to be relaying his orders, were clearly at loggerheads because few of the instructions ever filtered through to us.

Filming with a rostrum camera, a floor camera and a

crane camera, and having all the hassle of a day spent slithering about on ice, breathing acrid smoke and coping with the monotonous repetition of take after take, all to create Hell, certainly worked in so far as it was purgatory for everyone concerned. I said as much in the dressing-room afterwards, when the girl was peeling off the horns. 'Yes,' she said, 'but think of the money, dear. You can laugh all the way to the bank.'

I thought afterwards, she's right. I earned more for this one day's work than I ever earned on a Carry On film, and they took six to eight weeks to shoot.

5 October

Had to rise very early and rush to Marylebone station in order to get to the school in Buckinghamshire where I was giving a talk. The first-class fare is a fraud. The accommodation seemed little different from that provided in second-class.

One of the masters met me at the station, and drove me to the school. 'You can leave your coat in the lavatory,' he said as he showed me in, and opened the door to the WC.

'Isn't there somewhere more private?' I asked, and he reluctantly showed me to the headmaster's office. The head then appeared, his chief characteristic seeming to be an ability to mispronounce words like 'municipal' as 'moony-sippal'. 'We're having lunch, a cold boofay', he said, 'we'll join you later.' They did and introduced me to a lady who'd worked in hospitals in the Emirates.

She said, 'I'm afraid I'll have to leave during your talk,' and the headmaster said, 'So will I. I've got papers to mark.' It was all very discouraging. My morale was round my ankles.

I was shown into the school theatre where there was a

packed house and I blundered through the script, reading very badly, because I'd forgotten to bring my spectacles. It wasn't a success, I'm afraid, unlike my time at Eton, when I went like a bomb, having remembered my glasses.

One boy at Eton rose at question-time and asked, 'How do you manage to look so young?' After that I've had nothing but admiration for everyone at the school. When I departed I said to the headboy, 'It did go rather well. Who did you have last week?'

'Sir Robert Mark.'

'How did he go?' I asked.

'Well, put it this way,' was the reply, 'they applauded him, but they gave you a standing ovation.'

Alas it wasn't so today. Perhaps I'm looking older. Consoled myself with Firbank's line: 'When the last crow's foot falls into place, one achieves a certain peace.'

7 October

Went to the TV Centre to do a show and one of the actors was complaining about the fear of losing his voice. 'Just imagine opening your mouth and only being able to croak.'

The announcer said drily, 'Pop singers don't have to imagine.'

Tried to rest in the dressing-room, but was disturbed by the noise from workmen. I went out into the corridor and remonstrated, 'Some people are trying to sleep before the show.'

One of the men quipped. 'Never mind, Kenny. With you, they can sleep while it's on.'

10 October

To dinner at Harry Nuttall's where the conversation turned to impersonations. One of the guests related a story in the papers about a man dressing up as an Arab Sheikh in order to impress the town with his 'oil wealth' and the local Chamber of Commerce obtaining kudos from his exploits.

Harry's own story, however, was even better. He said that he knew of a scion of a noble family, many years ago, who did brilliant impersonations of Queen Mary. He would alight from a very old Daimler, with a ramrod back and dressed appropriately, with a toque, a pearl choker and holding a stick. The chauffeur would ring the bell of whichever house they were visiting and announce, 'Her Majesty has arrived'. The occupants were always full of awe and delight, because the Queen was renowned for calling unexpectedly. This impersonator always called at four o'clock so people hurried to get out their very best china and arrange a royal tea-party. Any objet d'art that caught his eye which he admired was always offered to him, and he collected an impressive haul from his hosts' desire to win favour at court.

'On one occasion,' Harry said, 'the visit went terribly wrong. The Daimler pulled up outside a house in Chester Square. The old chauffeur went through the usual routine, knocked on the door and said, 'The Queen has arrived.'

The butler told him curtly, 'Go away, you fool, she's already here.'

12 October

To Selfridges in search of a Letts A4 diary for next year. If you don't go early, they're gone. Found one that I liked but complained to the girl about the marks on the binding. 'Well, you can have it at £6,' she said. 'The original price was £6.40.' I felt I'd pulled off a tremendous coup.

Then I went to the basement where I saw a man demonstrating a magnetic window-cleaner, which ingeniously clamped itself to the glass and cleaned both sides simultaneously. I was enormously impressed, but determined to be cautious. I thought I'd ask a few questions before making the purchase. I said to the demonstrator, 'What happens if the pad wears out?'

'We sell you a replacement, sir.'

'How much is the whole appliance?'

'£4.75.'

'Oh dear, that is very expensive.'

'On the contrary, sir, less than you'd pay a window-cleaner.'

'Yes . . . that is true. But on the other hand, you are demonstrating on a huge piece of glass, aren't you?'

'That shows you, sir, how much you can clean in such a short time.'

'But I've got very small panes,'

'In that case, sir, I should see a doctor.'

I affected amusement, but I was secretly furious with the giggling and nudging of the crowd, so I beat a dignified retreat.

All shopping is beset with trouble. I was told once about an exclusive London emporium, where an irate customer, appalled at the price of Beluga caviar, told the assistant where to put it. 'I'd be delighted to oblige you, sir,' came the quick-witted but respectful reply, 'but I am already accommodating a two-guinea cucumber.' Whether it's true or not, it does typify an unhappy aspect of modern shopping: how does one get what one wants at the price one can afford? I've bitten my nails outside shop windows and gone round the block and back again before plucking up enough courage to go in and actually buy something. I'm always irritated if the goods don't carry a price tag. I don't want the embarrassment of asking how much and then learning I can't afford it.

I'm neither clever enough nor far-sighted enough to carry notes about measurements of everything. I don't know my inside leg from an outside right, and I frequently confuse the collar size with the neckband. When I get the things home and discover my error, I seldom have the courage to explain the mistake. I just give up. Some people, however, go back endlessly. Rona Anderson (Gordon Jackson's wife) changed her bed five times and she got the first one in a sale! The assistant was practically demented by her fourth complaint about the mattress and only avoided a breakdown by taking his annual holiday two weeks earlier than usual. He left a hapless junior to deal with this loquacious and exuberant blonde who seemed blissfully unaware of time. Rona will wax eloquent about orthopaedic beds until the cows come home; not that cows have anything to do with beds — chairs, yes! In the past cows were responsible for a lot of upholstery in that department. People would say, 'real cow-hide' in reverent tones, and the possessor of a genuine leather chair felt his position was elevated in more than one sense.

That's all been altered now by PVC. The rubbish is so artfully produced that it often looks like leather. You don't know the difference until you sit on it, and then your enlightenment isn't pleasant. Real leather doesn't leave your trousers sticking to your behind. PVC does. Barry Wade has an eagle-eye and is never deceived by simulation; whenever he detects the stuff, he objects. In a restaurant, if he discovers PVC upholstery, he carefully covers the seat with a napkin before settling down to a meal. He always says, 'You can't beat leather', though Spanish tooling and rodeos provide startling evidence to the contrary.

141

In fact I met someone who told me, 'Horse saddles are so comfortable, you can go to sleep in them!' Not that anyone would, of course. Not that anyone *could*. You don't have leather beds, not unless you're eccentric. I've not seen any leather beds in deaprtment stores. They don't make them, or if they do, they haven't told me.

Mind you, the things they haven't told me are legion, like a preparation for the over-hirsute, which, I was told, removed unwanted hair. They didn't tell me it removed half your skin as well. In the end I was resorting to hormone creams, hydrocortisone, not to mention Queen's royal jelly – well, frankly, it isn't worth mentioning unless you're mad about bees, and apart from a teaspoonful of honey on the odd occasion, I can take or leave bees: preferably in a very large apiary veil.

14 October

Went to Capital Radio for the Michael Aspel show. I'm doing a piece on newspaper cuttings of my choice. Roughed out my bits half-an-hour beforehand. Went on and did it without fluffing. After that, it was a day of shopping again. I got my envelopes at the stationers. Then the ex-milkman appeared at the door and said, 'I've been suspended because there have been complaints about me. Would you write me a testimonial?'

I said, 'Certainly I will. You've always given me good service.' So I sat down and wrote a fulsome and very complimentary letter. He thanked me profusely, but his whisky-laden breath made me realize why he hadn't lingered long at the dairy.

Then I went to Boots to get some vitamin pills. On to Woolworths and found Knight's Castile soap at sixteen pence. Grabbed six tablets hurriedly, thinking this offer may not last very long. I want it because my initials (K.C. for Kenneth Charles) on the soap never fail to impress visitors to my bathroom.

16 October

People have extraordinary ideas about the way actors live. While cleaning the windows the woman in the flat above saw me from the street. When I passed her on the stairs she said, 'I couldn't believe my eyes when I saw you cleaning the windows.'

'Why?' I asked.

'Well,' she said, 'I thought you'd have someone in.'

I went round to Mount Street, where Ingrid Bergman has a flat, and found her on a ladder, washing down the walls of her kitchen. Falling into the same error as my neighbour I asked. 'Why don't you get someone in to do this?'

To which she replied, 'If you want something done properly, you've got to do it yourself.' Then she said, 'Hang on, I won't take a minute.' She came down from the ladder and within ten minutes brought to the table Swedish meat balls with a salad, a most piquant dressing, and a bottle of chilled white wine. One would have thought that the house was staffed by *cordon bleu* cooks, vintners and a whole army of char women instead of one renowned actress, alas now no more, fresh from her wall-washing.

17 October

Maudie Fittleworth told me a bizarre story about being on Waterloo station when a train was pulling out and three dreadful drunks rushed through the barrier. She said, 'I called to the porter, "Let's give them a hand." They were all practically incapable. We managed to get two of them on and then the train pulled out. I turned to the one that was left – well, bent down to him actually because he was prostrate – and said, "I'm sorry, we couldn't get you on the train." And the drunk said, "My friends will be sorry too. They were seeing me off." '

I said, 'Really, Maudie, that story's very old.'

She said, 'So are your legs, but they're still getting you around.'

19 October

Walked to Euston and got the 9.35 to Birmingham, where I demonstrated cooking on *Pebble Mill at One*. I made a Spanish omelette. I broke the eggs expertly into a jug, whisked them, pointed out to the audience that you must get them into a fluffy consistency. Then I took handfuls of vegetables and bits of meat, saying, 'Whatever's left over at the weekend, just shove it all in. The whole point about a Spanish omelette is that it can contain anything.' When I went to lift it out of the pan, it split. There was a lot of laughter and I said, 'Oh, no, there's no need to laugh or deride my efforts. This is supposed to split. It is a collapsible Spanish omelette' – which I thought was very quick of me.

22 October

Went to do *Give Us A Clue* at Teddington. I appeared on the team with Gareth Hunt and Lonnie Donegan. Hung around until nine o'clock before we started.

Nanette Newman was appearing on the women's side and she said to me, 'Do you remember when we travelled up to Manchester together? That man in the carriage was reading *The Times* and you pulled it down from his face and said, "Oh, leave that, dear, our conversation will be much more interesting." '

I said, 'No, I don't remember that at all.'

'Well, you did.'

It is extraordinary how we all gain different impressions of each other. I'm sure I never did such a thing.

Gareth Hunt said, 'The money in advertising is so good, you feel almost sinful when you are taking it.'

As I've just been playing the Devil in the advert, it certainly struck a responsive chord.

26 October

To Manchester for a pilot show of a new panel game with Russell Harty. We had to act scenes incorporating into our ad-libbing a phrase that we were given beforehand. One girl had the line 'blood is thicker than water'. She was supposed to be on a desert island, where Lance Percival was washed up and found her. Two coconuts fell from the palm tree under which she was sitting. She picked them up while she was ad-libbing and said, 'You won't be without nutrition here. I've got a couple full of milk.' The audience fell about laughing and I honestly don't think the girl meant it rudely at all. She was an innocent young child, but since she had an ample bosom and was looking at Lance Percival as she said it, it all had connotations which were not at all envisaged by the management.

Afterwards we were taken back to our hotels and I was put in the Grand. I didn't find it grand at all. When I sat on the loo, the seat fell on my back and cut my spine. I complained to the manager, who said, 'You're supposed to sit on the seat.'

'No, I always sit on the porcelain,' I told him.

'Well, that's most unusual.'

'I'm not concerned whether it's usual or not, I'm concerned with the fact that the seat fell forward and struck me on the back. Also, there wasn't a coat-hanger to be seen. There were masses of settees, cocktail cabinets and coffee tables in the room, but not one sign of a coat-hanger.'

'No, we simply put a bed in the lounge,' he said. 'You were occupying part of a suite.'

'Well,' I returned spiritedly, 'Your suite has left me very sour. I think you're taking money under false pretences.'

28 October

Jonathan James-Moore telephoned apropos of David Hatch's departure as producer of *Just A Minute*: 'There will be a party afterwards to wish him *bon voyage*, and I wondered if you would like to say a few words?'

I very nearly asked, 'In sixty seconds?', but I simply said I'd be pleased to pay tribute to David, because the show owes a great debt to him. He has ensured its long-running success.

At the party, Jonathan told me about two people commenting on Mrs Thatcher's arrival at the Tory party conference, superbly attired in a very chic outfit. One remarked, 'Immaculate,' and other replied, 'Yes, but absolutely no conception.'

November

2 November

Went to do a voice-over for a commercial featuring two cherubs. They'd booked me for one voice and Hugh Paddick for the other. Hugh didn't turn up. They telephoned him and were told he was in bed and could think of no excuse to get out. So they said they'd have to cancel the session and I said, 'No! I'll do both voices.' So I did one as Noël Coward and one as the 'stop messing about' character. They were very pleased.

I met Henry Cooper and Kevin Keegan there doing their Brut commercial. Kevin said, 'You remember the night we all went to that trattoria in Notting Hill Gate? It was terribly generous of you to give us such a wonderful meal.'

'Not at all,' I said, 'I believe in largesse, especially in times of recession.'

It was only when I left that I realized my agent had paid the bill. Nevertheless I do think it's important to give an *impression* of generosity in hard times.

8 November

Dinner at Gordon and Rona's. One of their guests told us about an impoverished actress who frequently accompanied Dame Edith Evans on social occasions. Edith would pick her up in a hired car and take her to dinner. The impecunious actress – who always complained about having to make do with shoddy clothing – would talk of her sewing skill which ensured she had a presentable wardrobe.

Then she landed a commercial in which she was portraying a very grand lady, presiding at a supper table, eating some famous chocolate mints. The wardrobe had fitted her with a very expensive gown and after the filming she was told she could keep it. On the next occasion when Edith arrived to collect her, she entered the limousine, rustling in the silks of her new-found *haute couture*. The Dame's eyes widened in surprise and when the usual courtesies had been exchanged, the famous tones boomed querulously, 'Don't tell me you ran that up yourself.'

9 November

Went to a crowded Fortnum and Mason to get a Christmas pudding, Aunt Edith having announced with some asperity that she wasn't going to make them any more. There was such a queue at the pudding counter that I went to another and said to the assistant, who was free, 'I can't hang about. There are crowds trying to get Christmas puddings. Could you fiddle me one?'

'Hang on,' he said, and ran off to the other counter. He returned with the pudding and rang it up on his own till.

'Impatient little imp, aren't you?' he said.

'You can say that again,' I laughed, but unfortunately he did.

11 November

Democracy has gone mad. I went to Audio International to do a recording and the girl in reception asked, 'What name?'

I said, 'I would have thought that with my face that sort of question would hardly be necessary.'

'I don't know your name.'

'I don't know yours.'

'Well, I've got to announce you, what shall I say?'

'Call me Kenneth . . . and I'll try and think of something to call you.'

16 November

To the Paris Studio for *Just A Minute* with Nicholas Parsons, Tim Rice, John Junkin and Brian Johnston. Before we went on I said to Tim Rice, 'Oh heavens, it's an all-male panel.'

He looked at me witheringly and said, 'Well, *al*most.'

When I went on, I told the audience what he'd said. They fell about.

I was given some appalling subjects, including Quetzalcoatl. Not knowing very much about Mexican mythology, I decided to concentrate on the Quetzal part of the word, and said that it was a South American bird with exotic plumage and that the distinguished ornithologist, Ludwig Koch, was offered a sighting of this rare bird, but it entailed spending an entire night in the Peruvian rain forest, and he uttered that immoral phrase, 'I'm not getting wet for a load of bleeding birds.' I was pulled up in the midst of this dissertation by one of the contestants who said it was deviation and nothing to do with the truth, nor with Quetzalcoatl. Parsons agreed.

'You ignorant great fool,' I cried out in protest. 'You know nothing about it either. You're no authority on Mexican mythology. You couldn't run a whelk-stall, let alone a panel game, you ignorant nit.'

He said, 'Really, Kenneth, I don't know how you can carry on in this way. I couldn't talk like that.'

To which I replied, 'Of course you couldn't, you haven't got my vocabulary.'

In the ensuing laughter I smirked triumphantly.

18 November

Letter came this morning from Peter Nichols, saying there were plans for making his play *Privates on Parade* into a film.

I wrote back saying that I hoped he would be able to get in all the eccentric events, including the extraordinary moment when the ballet dancer met the brigadier outside the HQ in Singapore. He did three pirouettes in front of this slack-jawed blimp and tapped him on the shoulder crying, 'Tell your mother we're here, dear, and put the kettle on.' An embarrassed aide explained to the officer, 'He's part of a group of troop entertainers, sir. They've been sent out from London.'

'I should think the city was damned glad to get rid of them,' snorted the brigadier, expressing that deep divide 'twixt army and theatre.

20 November

To the Paris again for *Just A Minute* and told Sheila Hancock about doing *Quote Unquote* in the same studio where John Lahr told us that his father, Bert, used to say, 'The light at the end of the tunnel may be an oncoming train.' She found that very amusing.

I told her a story of Stanley Baxter's when he got into conversation with a taxi driver on one occasion. The driver told Stanley about seeing Harold Wilson on television. 'Did you see it, Stan?' he asked.

'No, I didn't.'

'Oh, he was very amiable; very fail hello, well met.'

We all laughed at the quite unintended perceptiveness of the spoonerism.

21 November

Saw Michael for dinner. He asked how the last *Just A Minute* went. I told him, 'When I mentioned that I'd used witch-hazel cream for ten years, Peter Jones said, "And to no effect whatsoever", which got a huge laugh.'

Michael said, 'Your skin looks all right to me.'

'Ah, yes,' I replied, 'but then it was ablaze with acne.'

I also told him that Parsons had remarked, 'Part of my schooling was in Scotland.'

Clement Freud commented, 'You mean you're only half-educated?'

Michael asked, 'Will that go in your diary.'

'Of course,' I said. 'It already contains two of your *bon mots*.'

'Then I shall be in very distinguished company.'

'I wouldn't be too sure about that,' I said. 'Maudie's in it too.'

He looked crestfallen, so I picked up the bill.

23 November

Up to Leeds for a literary luncheon at the university. I dwelt upon the resilient nature of our island race and its ability to succour persecuted minorities. In conclusion I quoted the Clemence Dane lines:

> Then came exiles who fled from death,
> Hunted Huguenots, Jews from Spain,
> To the wise island; drew sobbing breath
> In easy air and smelled the may,
> Sweet as a kiss on a summer day.

Oh, with such pride,
People have lived and died
For this country of cornfield and briar rose,
Buttercup meadow and orchard close;
England, the people's England,
The welcoming land.

Several people afterwards asked me the name of the author.
I told them it was Clemence Dane and one of the publishers'
representatives present told me that it was a pseudonym. I
looked it up afterwards and found it was true. Her real
name was Winifred Ashton.

24 November

To Equity Council meeting. Mostly routine matters. The
Theatre Secretary asked me if I would be free for a
TMA (Theatre Managers' Association) meeting, and I hastily said, 'Oh no, I'm up to my eyes in it,' as if I was sinking
into quagmire. In truth, I could attend, but I remember the
last occasion being endlessly tedious. The only bright
moment came after a long and boring statement, when
Michael Codron leant across and whispered, 'If this show
ever comes to town, it'll have to be cut.'

25 November

Going through some old papers, I found the transcript
of an *Any Questions* programme that I'd been on in
1973. Reading the script reminds me of how the impromptu
remark uttered without due regard for other people's feelings can rebound on one. During a discussion on co-
educational schools, they asked about my childhood deal-
ings with the opposite sex and I replied, 'My experience is

most unfortunate in this line. I was once mad about a girl called Iris Jerome. She used to pee in the gutter and said it was all right to do so. She said that if you were caught short, the law did not frown on it.'

Nemesis was not slow in finding me out. A letter soon arrived saying, 'I heard you on *Any Questions*. I am the Iris Jerome you mentioned and I was appalled that you had to resuscitate the wet knickers of my youth.'

Strange how Iris turned up after all those years like a bad, not say spent, penny.

26 November

Stanley telephoned about meeting this afternoon 'You *will* be wearing a tie?' he asked.

'Of course,' I replied.

'Oh, good, only we can't enter my club without one. It was very embarrassing last week when a chum arrived in a very smart Dior blazer, but with an open-neck shirt. They won't allow that.'

When I met him there, he said, 'We'll have the toast and the Gentleman's Relish, it's quite delicious.'

He talked about his holiday plans. 'I feel a bit guilty about taking another trip abroad.'

'Rubbish,' I said, 'You deserve it. Think of all those years when you were struggling on the stage.'

'No, I did most of my struggling off-stage.'

Afterwards, we walked to the Plaza Cinema. On the way we passed a stooped figure, hunched over a carton of take-away food, garnished with French Fries. 'Oh, look,' Stanley said, 'It's Richard III With Chips.' I laughed immoderately.

27 November

I went to do a voice-over with an actress who smelled terribly of stale onions. No matter which way one turned, the odour was unavoidable. It reminded me of George Rose's experience playing with Noël Coward in *The Apple Cart*. 'I'd had *moules marinières*,' George explained, 'and didn't realize the garlic smelled so badly until I started playing the scene with Noël. He recoiled from me in horror and muttered, "Don't breathe out, you'll scorch the furniture polish." It was an aside, but quite audible. I nearly lost my lines, I was so taken aback. Then just as I was about to recover, he said, "We only need a little bread, and then we could all have a meal." After that, I was all over the place. When I came to the line asking for his abdication document, he ad-libbed outrageously, "Has that dreadful French maid hidden it behind the cushions? Let's look," and started scurrying all over the set in a ludicrous search for the paper. In the end, he suddenly whipped it out from his jacket. "Silly me, it was there all the time." '

When the actress with the bad breath had disappeared, I told the studio about George Rose's story and they asked, 'Did you ever meet Coward?'

'Yes, several times,' I said. 'The most memorable occasion was when he made an unexpected visit backstage to the Globe during the Shaffer play. When I thought that everyone had left the theatre, I procured a bowl of warm water, placed it on a chair and sat in it to wash my posterior. While I was on the bowl, there was a knock at the door. "Who is it?" I asked.

A voice said, "Noël."

I thought it was somebody in the company larking about and said, "Go away." But the door opened, Coward appeared and I shot up, knocking the bowl of water all over the floor.

155

"What on earth are you doing?" he asked. I told him as delicately as I could and he replied immediately, "Oh my dear, it's piles. Of course, I know all about the suffering involved. Have you read my account in *Present Indicative*?"

"No," I said defensively. "I've never had piles. I do have papilli."

"Papilli?" he said. "My dear, it's an island in the South Seas."

I later found that indeed it was.'

28 November

Called on Alyn Ainsworth, who told me he'd been burgled. I said the same thing had happened to me. 'They took two pairs of shoes. They took my socks. They even took my old underpants.'

Alyn said, 'They'd have fetched a fortune at Sothebys.'

The guests at dinner included David Bell and Bruce McLure, who are chums of Stanley Baxter's, so we had a lot in common. I related the saga of the old man standing outside the chemist, croaking out a tale of woe to Stanley. 'My first wife took ages dying and I had to nurse her. It was awful. Then I met my second wife and I asked her if she was robust (he pronounced it "roe bust") and she swore she was, went down on her knees and said, "Yes, Fred. I am robust. I am hale and hearty." So I married her and what happened? Tuberculosis within six weeks. I was at it all over again. Nursing, nursing, I got sick of it. Mind you, she was a lovely woman. I've got reels of film I took of her with my Kodak Brownie. Lovely shots, none of your *Vogue* magazine rubbish. Beautiful colouring she had. But I can't afford to get them developed, not on my pension.'

Stanley offered him a fiver so that he could have them

developed. 'Get out of it,' cried the old man. 'Get out of it,' he said again, refusing the money with an imperious sweep of the hand. 'A fiver . . . that'd never cover it.'

December

1 December

I read in the paper they're still presenting the Dunmow Flitch. It's given annually to any couple proving conjugal harmony for a year and a day. The flitch is a whole side of a hog, apparently. It sounds very suspect to me. There must have been something wrong with it, because they say it's 'cured'. 'Cured' of what, one might ask? They won't tell you what illness it had; they try to make it sound acceptable by using phrases like 'home-cured', to give the impression that a lot of love has gone into it, that they have taken the poor hog into their home and lavished care and attention upon it. One thinks how charming and compassionate they must be, but no sooner is the pig out of its sick bed than they callously turn around and kill it. Then they slice it and shove it on the bacon counter in the supermarket.

A ministry inspector recently told me that hams have water added to them, quite unnecessarily. No one really knows what's going on half the time. If they tell you your television set's short-circuited with a faulty ferrite rod you don't know whether it's true or not. If you try to argue, you end up with lock-jaw.

I remember going to a specialist when I had an awful pain in my jaw. He asked me a lot of personal questions, which had nothing to do with my jaw. I think he was just being nosey. Then he sent me to a radiotherapy unit, where I was X-rayed. They muttered darkly about strained ligaments and then sent me to a dental surgeon. He said the teeth alignment affected the jaw and filed half my molars down. It didn't do any good, because I still had the pain in the jaw. I think he was just keeping his hand in.

Eventually I confided in the newspaper man outside Baker Street underground station. He said, 'Shut your mouth.'

'I beg your pardon?'

'I said shut your mouth. Tie a scarf round your head and go to bed.'

I took his advice and, sure enough, in the morning the pain had gone. When I saw him I told him, 'I never expected you'd succeed where all those so-called wise men had failed.'

He said to me, 'It's like the Bible says, "Out of the mouths of babes and newsvendors".'

I agreed, but left thinking that while he may know something about biology, he's a bit dodgy on theology.

2 December

Passed number 9 Cork Street today, where my old agent, Peter Eade, once had his office. I must have toiled up those stairs hundreds of times. He was a dear man with an avuncular attitude, always ready with a sympathetic ear in times of adversity. I took Rachel Roberts to his office in 1951, after meeting her in rep in Swansea. She was worried about what to wear. She'd been working at the Ideal Home exhibition and they'd lent her a red velvet frock for the job. She wanted to know if she should come in it. It was quite a few years afterwards that Peter proudly announced he'd got her the highest salary for a leading lady in the West End, when she starred in *Maggie May* at the Adelphi. She could wear what she liked then.

I always remember dining with Rachel at La Cupole when she argued against my asexual nature. 'You shouldn't condemn promiscuity', she said.

I said it led to wasted aims, but she argued, 'No, it's better to experience *something*. Your life is lived entirely on a fantasy level. You've no real knowledge of people.'

'Oh I have', I told her. 'I look at their faces, especially when they're unaware of being watched. I see the lines of tiredness and think they could be out of a medieval canvas. As far as I'm concerned, their faces are all works of art. Like other precious objects, they're to be admired, but not touched.'

Rachel was unpersuaded. To the end, for her, the heart would always rule the head.

4 December

After *Just A Minute* tonight, I took Clement Freud aside and asked him, 'I've got to speak at a lunch soon, what can I say?'

'Criticize the menu, it works like a dream. They always give you the same old things, so comment on that. "Your menu is very unadventurous: dreary prawn cocktail to start with — why couldn't you have shown a little imagination? Half a dozen oysters would have been delightful." '

'Aren't oysters an aphrodisiac?' I asked.

'Oh yes,' said Clement, 'if you don't swallow them quickly, your neck goes stiff.'

I laughed but secretly thought it was hardly suitable for a luncheon with literary *aficionados*.

6 December

Making some notes for my radio talk with Frank Topping, I re-read Shakespeare's words: 'They say miracles are past and we have our philosophical persons to make modern and familiar things supernatural and cause-less. Hence it is that we make trifles of errors, ensconcing ourselves in seeming knowledge, when we should submit ourselves to an unknown fear.'

What a modern ring the words possess, and what

significance for us today. Extraordinary that they were written hundreds of years ago. The bit about 'ensconcing ourselves in seeming knowledge' is applicable to so much. Our lives are becoming dominated by technical complexity. Indeed some people seem to believe in technology itself. You actually hear fallacious rubbish like, 'It was the fault of the computer'. This sort of line is trotted out as if it were a reasonable explanation. And when Shakespeare says, 'we should submit ourselves to an unknown fear', he expresses an aspect of faith natural to a Tudor mind, but fast vanishing from twentieth-century thought. The unknown is mysterious and it's in the acknowledging of the mystery that faith begins. Modern intelligence objects strongly and prefers to denigrate what it can't analyse, seeking refuge in science and so-called facts.

Only love is deep enough to plumb the depths of the unfathomable. Many who reject faith so readily, dismissing it as meaningless mumbo-jumbo, find nothing odd about consulting the astrology columns. They're quite happy to accept the star signs and horoscopes from people who use a jargon that is vague to the point of lunacy. Marty Feldman used it in *Round the Horne*, when he gave Madam Osiris the line, 'Your lucky sandwich-filling is salmon and shrimp. Your lucky stone is gall. And Uranus is in its last stages.'

7 December

Walking back from depositing tax money in the building society, I met Bamber Gascoine in Museum Street. I told him I'd seen *University Challenge* the week before and he surprised me by saying that it had been on for fifteen years.

'Goodness, is it that long?' I asked.

'Yes,' he said, 'almost as long as your *Just A Minute*.'

163

'Oh, that does make me feel old.'

Then we fell to talking about *Share My Lettuce*, which he wrote. I said, 'The dialogue I always remember was in that tea-party with Maggie Smith, when I played the nervous visitor, watching the coloured balls roll out from under the table, while Maggie poured the tea, impervious to these untoward occurrences.

I had to say, "These balls keep coming out from under the table". Her line in reply was an icy, "We don't talk about that", and then she asked, "Have I got a goitre hanging from the side of my neck with hairs sprouting from it?" When I answered, "Yes", she said, "Quite so, we don't talk about that either." '

More than two decades later, we both still chuckled at the memory.

10 December

With Louie to do some shopping in the Edgware Road. We passed a poster announcing the opening of a Lebanese restaurant and she said, 'Oh, they're opening another of those Lesbian places.'

'*Lebanese*,' I told her.

She nodded. 'That's right. They're all over the place now. It's all very outspoken, quite different from when I was a girl.'

When decimal currency came in, Louie would keep saying, 'I can't get used to this dismal money', and all corrections were to no avail.

'It's decimal, not dismal', I kept telling her. 'Don't you want to get it right?'

She said, 'I am right. As far as I'm concerned, it's dismal.'

11 December

Maudie Fittleworth rang and told me a cure for deafness is to press your fingers into the ears very hard and then release them. 'Oh,' I said, 'good job it's not a cure for piles.'

14 December

Went to the Paris Studio for *Just A Minute*. There was a queue even in this dreadful weather. During the game, Parsons rebuked me, 'Your diction is appalling.'

I replied, 'It's as good as yours, when you've got your teeth in,' and thankfully, the audience laughed.

Then I was given 'paper tearing' as my topic for sixty seconds and I said, 'I've only done this in the smallest room in the house.'

Parsons got all the names and marks wrong and I shouted, 'He doesn't want a desk-chair, he wants a bath-chair. They carry him in here, you know. Oh yes, they have to inject him before he goes on. They pump all this Queen's Royal Jelly into him. They tried monkey glands, but he had a surplus.'

Oh, the rudeness into which the ad-lib leads us!

15 December

Dread the idea of tonight's party, full of people I don't know. You're supposed to be shepherded around and introduced, but hosts frequently desert you in your hour of need and I always find it disconcerting. I try to look nonchalant, smoke fags in a sophisticated fashion and affect an interest in pictures on the wall, but can never think of a bright opening sally. What does one say to strangers? Stanley Baxter once remarked 'Oh it's easy! You simply say a line from any popular song. It works like a dream. Do it with enough profundity, it sounds marvellous. Only recently at a party, I sailed up to this woman and said, "Moonlight becomes you, it goes with your hair", and she was obviously delighted, conversation flowed and the whole thing went like a bomb.'

I took his advice. At the party I found myself standing next to a morose-looking American and smiled gaily, plunging straight in with, 'I like New York in June, how about you?'

He leered and said, 'I like it anytime of the year,' and launched into some prurient details about his escapades in that city.

I wish I'd never started the conversation at all. Other people's recipes are not always beneficial.

16 December

Went to Barry Wade's party this evening, where at least I knew some people. I said to Nicky Luton, 'You're a dead ringer for James Dean. You bear an extraordinary resemblance to him.'

He didn't look at all pleased. 'Don't you think that's a compliment?' I asked.

'No,' he said, 'I don't want to be compared with anybody.'

It's funny, we never learn; none of us likes to be compared with anyone else. When I went on the set of *The Beggar's Opera*, Laurence Olivier said to Peter Brook, 'Look at his face, he looks exactly like Jean-Louis Barrault.' Wondering what he looked like, I shot off to see *Les Enfants du Paradis* and felt far from flattered when I saw this white-faced aesthete on the screen. I didn't warm to Barrault at all until I read what he had said to Peter Hall apropos of the subsidized national theatre: 'May I tell you an anecdote? Molière wrote *Le Misanthrope*, a half-success. The suffering of Alceste was not in keeping with Molière's reputation as a humorist. Seeing the disaster coming, within a period of ten days Molière wrote *Le Medecin malgré lui*, to pursue its eternal road. If he had been comfortably subsidized, would Molière have felt the need to write *Le Médecin malgré lui?* which he attached to *Le Misanthrope* as one would pull the liner *Queen Elizabeth* with a small tug. A great success! After that *Le Misanthrope* was no longer in need of its small tug, *Le Médecin malgré lui*. The dangerous life and the pay at the end of the month have their uses.'

17 December

Went to the hospital and saw Mr Mulvaney and said, 'The bum is terribly painful.'

He examined me and said, 'You've a small pile, just inside the entrance. I'll have to inject it. It'll be like trying to stab a moving curtain because the tissue is so fine.' I didn't feel anything in the event and it was all quite painless and when I was dressing, he said, 'You're in very good company, you know. Napoleon couldn't mount his horse at Waterloo, he had the most dreadful piles.'

'Well, I've played the role,' I said, 'don't tell me about Napoleon's illnesses. I played him in the TV production of Anouilh's *French Cricket*. It was set during Napoleon's return from Elba when he was suffering from cancer of the stomach. I was provided with a large amount of cotton wool to stuff down my trousers to make a protuberance. During the play the wadding moved, so that by the end, instead of a protuberant stomach, I had a huge bum. I asked the producer if we could shoot the last scene again, but he said, "No, no, don't worry about a thing. It all looked thoroughly authentic. I thought it was part of your characterization and that towards the end of the play you'd developed dropsy as well."

I fancied this was the producer's subtle version of the bum's rush.'

18 December

Felt much more comfortable this morning and remembered the occasion when, after one *Hancock's Half-Hour*, I went with Tony, Sid James and Jack Train to a chemist and we each asked for a packet of suppositories, the man looked with increasing incredulity at each face, and asked, 'Is this some sort of joke?'

Jack Train told him, 'Believe me, mate, I only wish it were.'

I fancy he'd never had such an illustrious line-up for piles.

19 December

This Christmas I'm really getting a showing. I'm on the Michael Parkinson compilation. There's a Carry On. I'm on Capital Radio. And I'm on BBC television doing *Willo-the-Wisp* for children's hour. This project began two years ago. I looked up the entry in my diary where I noted the difficulty I was having with the multiplicity of voices required. 'I sounded like a strangulated soprano for Evil Edna, but on hearing the playback I laughed immoderately.' Read it aloud to Louie who said, 'Well, it doesn't take much to get you going.'

22 December

To Equity Council meeting. In a coffee break Greta Gouriet sweetly asked, 'Would you like to come to dinner with your mum?'

I said, 'Oh yes, where do you live?' and reached for pencil and paper.

'Hampton Court,' she said.

I swiftly recanted. 'No thank you. Dinner is one thing, but journeying to the country is quite another.'

Read a charming account in the paper about Mrs Runcie, wife of the Archbishop of Canterbury, attending a school display, depicting the nativity in the Bethlehem stable. A small boy talked to her about there being no room at the inn and said, 'I blame Joseph; he should have booked.'

23 December

By chance walked past Park West, the building where I used to live. It is full of curious memories for me. It was in a sixth-floor apartment there that I met Hal Roach, veteran director of Laurel and Hardy films, when he was toying with the idea of making an American slapstick series. He was a plump and merry little man and outlined his scenario with great enthusiasm. 'There's this very funny scene where you're seated on a newly-painted lavatory-seat and we have a lot of gags with the cistern overflowing. The water shoots up your behind and when you get up, the wooden seat is stuck to your ass. How about that!' He wheezed with uproarious laughter. 'A lavatory seat, stuck to your ass!' He was still laughing when I left.

It was in the same building that I met Eric Miller, who was then head of Peachey Property Corporation, which owned the block. He was knighted under the Wilson administration. I was a tenant on the second floor and complained to Eric about noisy parties being given in the adjacent apartment. 'One is kept up half the night,' I told him.

At the time he seemed to be listening with half an ear, for his head was turned for a profile view to a sculptress, who was moulding a clay model of his head. 'Do you think this is vain of me?' he asked, and was obviously more concerned with the bronze bust than with my noisy neighbours.

Then, suddenly, out of the blue, he said, 'Do you remember old Hawkins the maths master at Stanley Central?'

'Who could ever forget him?' I countered. 'But how do you know about a maths master at my old school?'

'I was there with you,' he told me. 'Remember the group of us attired in lederhosen at County Hall, when we sang *Die Himmel Ruhmen*.'

'Oh yes,' I replied. 'I've got the group photograph in my album.'

'Next time you open it, take a look at the boy on your right,' he said.

As soon as I got home, I did just that. The dark-haired cherub beside me was Eric Miller all right, but the picture bore little resemblance to the chairman of the board of Peachey Property. Since his untimely death, the company has sold the Park West, though in the old days it boasted a swimming pool, a restaurant and a bar.

It was there, too, that I had a reunion with Babette O'Deal. I hadn't seen her since the disastrous tour of *High and Low*, when she had to leave the show in Rangoon, because of an indisposition. On the train journey in Burma, she'd foolishly accepted a slice of water-melon from a mendicant, though the M.O. had warned everyone that much of the local fruit was grown in typhus infested water.

During the opening number, she sang, 'It's A Grand Night For Singing' in between hurried visits to a makeshift commode in the wings of the theatre. The hapless chorus was left to fill in with their own impromptu version of the song, interspersed with her unexpected reappearance as she valiantly attempted to sing again. Most of the time, she picked up the melody in the wrong key and in the ensuing havoc, got a slow handclap from the bemused troop audience. One member of the cast wisecracked, 'With Babette O'Deal this show should run and run.'

24 December

Maudie Fittleworth rang very early this morning. 'Are you busy?'

'I'm in the middle of the crossword.'

'Oh that reminds me. What's a four letter word, ending in IT, meaning something you'd find in the bottom of a birdcage?'

'Grit.'

She fell about laughing and said she'd have to get a rubber.

'Is that what you rang me up about?'

'No, it's about Adrian and me. In the strictest confidence of course. Do you think it's right to have sex before marriage?'

'Not if it delays the ceremony.'

'No, really! We're both worried about it!'

'Because of the children?'

'Oh no, there's no danger of that. The doctor examined us both. He said Adrian has too much albumen and I have too much sugar. We can't have children, but we can make lovely meringues!'

Her ensuing cackle was so loud that I had to hold the

receiver away. When it stopped I asked, 'Are you really getting married?'

She said, 'If I were I shouldn't tell you! Mister Megaphone! It'd be all over London like a scandal smog!'

'That's very unkind, Maudie. At this hour I don't want to hear denigration. I need ego-massage.'

'Yes,' she cried. 'Like a reindeer needs a hatrack!' and rang off.

Sometimes I think she's strangely insensitive.

Went to the dairy for last-minute Christmas supplies, and pints and pints of long-life milk.

25 December

We steamed the pudding from Fortnum and Masons. It tasted absolutely delicious. We began with a glass of sherry and had wine with the meal. Washed up afterwards and found Louie was nodding off. I said, 'Come along now, the sun is out; we must walk in the park.' She protested, but I insisted and took her to the rose garden where the snow lay undisturbed everywhere. It was quite forlorn.

At tea-time got a frantic phone call from Maudie Fittleworth saying, 'Come round tonight, we'll have a marvellous do. I've got these plastic party novelties, a Michaelmas goose with mushrooms stuffed in the skin, chestnuts and at midnight a pair of doves are going to fly out of the chimney bearing a message of peace.'

'I'm afraid I can't, Maudie,' I lied, 'I've got another engagement.' She talks such rubbish. I happen to know she's got central heating and there isn't any aperture from which her harbingers of goodwill could erupt at any hour, let alone midnight.

When I told Louisa about the invitation from Maudie, she said: 'You should be going out to parties, not sitting at home, especially on a night like this! Everybody's celebrating.'

'No,' I told her, 'I'm not really interested in carousing and merry-making. I'd rather sit and read a book.'

'Yes, it's funny' she returned, 'but I never feel alone if I've got a good book. I always like to read in bed, I can't go to sleep straight away but after a few chapters I start nodding . . . that Jean Plaidy's very good . . . what are you reading?'

'Hugh Kingsmill'

'What's it about?'

'It's non-fiction; it's called *The Poisoned Crown*'

'Oh, non-fiction', she said disappointedly. 'I prefer a good story.'

After that, we watched Albert Finney being brilliant in an exciting film on television called *Loophole*. Then came the *Parkinson* compilation and I shuddered when I appeared – hair lank, bags under the eyes, cheeks sallow and prune-like. I said to Louisa, 'I look awful', but she disagreed vehemently: 'Of course you don't! That's a lovely suit and that's the shirt I ironed, isn't it?'. Sometimes I don't think Louie and I are discussing the same things.

Bade her goodnight and returned to my flat. The book was where I'd left it and I turned again to the page I'd marked with a postcard. In a few lines Hugh Kingsmill can encapsulate a series of thoughts with amazing clarity and perception. Poetry often does this; prose only rarely. But in *The Poisoned Crown* I found a superb example and must copy it out here in case the book ever gets mislaid; for this entry, it is a fitting conclusion:

> What is divine in man is elusive and impalpable, and he is easily tempted to embody it in a concrete form – a church, a country, a social system, a leader – so that he may realize it with less effort and serve it with more profit. Yet, as even Lincoln

proved, the attempt to externalise the kingdom of heaven in a temporal shape must end in disaster. It cannot be created by charters and constitutions nor established by arms. Those who set out for it alone will reach it together, and those who seek it in company will perish by themselves.

Index